MW01090071

Population-Based Survey Experiments

Population-Based Survey Experiments

DIANA C. MUTZ

PRINCETON UNIVERSITY PRESS

PRINCETON AND OXFORD

Published by Princeton University Press, 41 William Street,
Princeton, New Jersey 08540
In the United Kingdom: Princeton University Press, 6 Oxford
Street, Woodstock, Oxfordshire OX20 1TW
press.princeton.edu

Library of Congress Cataloging-in-Publication Data

Mutz, Diana Carole.
 Population-based survey experiments / Diana C. Mutz.
     p. cm.
 Includes bibliographical references and index.
 ISBN 978-0-691-14451-1 (hardback) — ISBN 978-0-691-14452-8 (pbk.)
1. Surveys—Methodology. 2. Social surveys—Methodology.   I. Title.

 HA31.2.M88 2011
 001.4'33—dc22

                                          2011002675

British Library Cataloging-in-Publication Data is available

This book has been composed in Utopia

Printed on acid-free paper. ∞

Printed in the United States of America

    3   5   7   9   10   8   6   4

Dedicated to my graduate students,

Who always remind me why this is fun

Contents

List of Tables

This book is intended to fill a gap in the literature on research methods in the social sciences. To date, methods textbooks have yet to formally incorporate population-based survey experiments into the repertoire of approaches that are taught to social scientists in training. Though this is likely to change in the not-too-distant future, for now my hope is that this volume will serve that purpose. Population-based survey experiments are not only useful as a tool for better understanding the social world; they also provide insight into the strengths and weaknesses of existing methods.

I owe my own enthusiasm and interest in population-based experiments to many different driving forces, but probably the first cause was Paul Sniderman. I had the good fortune to meet Paul during graduate school, but only came to know him well many years later in my career. In addition to championing this methodological approach, Paul served as a mentor to my career as well as the careers of many other scholars. He also planted the idea that I need not rely on secondary data for purposes of testing my research ideas, and thus encouraged me to pursue original data collection opportunities as frequently as possible.

After I participated in the early Multi-Investigator Study, it was Paul's idea to introduce me to Skip Lupia to talk about serving as co-Principal Investigators of future multi-investigator studies. This could not have been a better idea, because Skip could not have been a more generous collaborator. Undoubtedly, this was one of the smoothest and most enjoyable working relationships I have had. Together, during a year we shared at the Center for Advanced Study in the Behavioral Sciences, we hatched the idea for the proposal to the National Science Foundation for Time-sharing Experiments for the Social Sciences (TESS). After receiving the grant, we divided up the labor and plunged ahead, not quite knowing what to expect from the social science community.

The response was nothing short of wonderful, which is why I sincerely thank the National Science Foundation for the generous funding that brought TESS into being, and for their continued sponsorship. Although it probably distracted me from my own research agenda for quite a few years, the breadth of exposure that TESS gave me to other social science fields—at least a passing familiarity with fields far beyond my own—made it more than worthwhile. In addition, by observing how others made use of population-based survey experiments, my own work became stronger and more methodologically innovative. Further, my role in TESS afforded me the opportunity to play Santa Claus to more than a few struggling assistant professors and graduate students. Although I am not particularly fond of most administrative roles, it was the most rewarding kind of administrative work I can imagine.

The other character (and I do mean character) who was central in getting TESS off the ground was Pawandeep Lamba, who created the TESS online system at a time when we could find no good model to use for our online presence. Pawandeep not only set up the entire system in short order, he also learned to speak social science as a third language.

When I began organizing this book, the graduate students in my experimental design course helped tremendously in pointing out what did and did not make sense about many of the arguments I made. Most importantly, Susanna Dilliplane went over this manuscript with a fine tooth comb, eliminating jargon and contributing to a much smoother and more understandable presentation.

Last, but foremost, I thank the many scholars who submitted their original ideas to TESS for serving as pioneers in using this method and for educating me about its many possibilities. The novel ideas that people came up with for using the TESS platform were nothing short of spectacular, and they came simply from an open call to the social scientific community to make use of this new methodological approach. Without these many contributors, this book would not be possible. Although there are far too many to list individually here, I use many of their studies in the pages that follow to illustrate the tremendous potential of population-based experiments. In addition, links to their studies can be found in the TESS archives available online at http://tess.experimentcentral.org/previousstudies.html.

Because all TESS studies, including the raw data, the original proposals, and any conference papers or preliminary findings, become publicly available twelve months after the data are delivered to the investigators, the fruits of their many labors are also available in greater detail to anyone interested in making use of them. This deadline for proprietary use puts pressure on TESS investigators to publish their findings as soon as possible; however, whenever this has not happened, or wherever there are multiple studies to be mined in these data, the raw data are available for any social scientists to analyze. The online TESS archive allows social scientists to re-analyze one another's data or, in some cases, to use the same data for entirely different studies.

Some may want to use these archives for purposes of teaching experimental design or the analysis of experimental findings, while others may use them for purposes of fattening their CVs without waiting to collect fresh data. As a public resource, all of these uses are perfectly acceptable. In most cases in which I refer to a specific population-based experiment, I also reference the conference paper or publication in which a description of the analyses can be found. However, when I describe studies without providing a reference to the results, it is not for purposes of teasing readers or sending them running to hone their library skills. Some studies simply have not been mined yet and patiently await the investigator who will bring them to press.

Although times are changing and some question the long-term viability of representative samples of people collected through telephone interviews, or even those done via Internet, I am confident that some form of large-scale representative interview technology will exist for future generations of social scientists, whether it be phone-based, Internet-based, or based on some as-yet-unknown hybrid. For this reason, I believe that population-based survey experiments are here to stay. While social science experiments have long been a valuable national resource, the development of population-based experiments suggests that they can play an even more important role in the future. And most importantly, population-based experiments offer wonderful opportunities to innovate. It is toward encouraging this end that I hope this book makes its biggest contribution.

Population-Based Survey Experiments

Population-Based Survey Experiments

A HYBRID METHODOLOGY FOR THE SOCIAL SCIENCES

APPROACHES TO SCIENTIFIC knowledge are a bit like rabid sports rivals; often they cannot say anything nice about their own team without simultaneously disparaging the other side. At some level, they know these intense rivalries would not exist if the other team were not a worthy contender, but the positive aspects of the other side are seldom acknowledged.

Likewise, empirical social scientists tend to develop expertise either in large-scale observational methods such as survey research, or in laboratory-based experimental approaches. They then spend the rest of their careers defending their choice of that particular approach in virtually everything they publish. Each time we submit a journal article, we rehearse all of the advantages of our own methodological choice, briefly mention its weaknesses, and make the case in no uncertain terms that what we have spent our time on is worthwhile. Go team! Competition among methodological approaches is certainly implied, even if it is not explicitly stated. We do our best to defend our own ingroup by stressing the importance of internal validity if we have produced an experiment, or external validity if we have completed an observational study.

Fortunately, this caricature is gradually becoming less accurate, both in terms of its characterization of researchers—an increasing number of whom are trained in multiple methods—and in terms of how methodologists are focusing their attention. Although there are still many survey researchers working on improving their particular method, and many experimentalists focused on developing innovative experimental techniques, there are also methodologists paying specific attention to the problem of integrating results from experimental and observational studies. For the most part, these approaches involve applying complex statistical models to estimates of convenience sample-based experimental treatment effects in order to estimate what they might be in the population as a whole.[1] The goal of population-based experiments is to address this problem through research design rather than analyses, combining the best aspects of both approaches, capitalizing on their strengths and eliminating many of their

---

[1] See, for example, Sekhon (2009).

weaknesses. The purpose of this volume is to introduce scholars and students in the social sciences to the possibilities of this approach.

Defined in the most rudimentary terms, a population-based survey experiment is an experiment that is administered to a representative population sample. Another common term for this approach is simply "survey-experiment," but this abbreviated form can be misleading because it is not always clear what the term "survey" is meant to convey. The use of survey methods does not distinguish this approach from other combinations of survey and experimental methods. After all, many experiments already involve survey methods at least in administering pre-test and post-test questionnaires, but that is not what is meant here. Population-based survey experiments are not defined by their use of survey interview techniques—whether written or oral—nor by their location in a setting other than a laboratory. Instead, a population-based experiment[2] uses survey *sampling* methods to produce a collection of experimental subjects that is representative of the target population of interest for a particular theory, whether that population is a country, a state, an ethnic group, or some other subgroup. The population represented by the sample should be representative of the population to which the researcher intends to extend his or her findings.

In population-based survey experiments, experimental subjects are randomly assigned to conditions by the researcher, and treatments are administered as in any other experiment. But the participants are not generally required to show up in a laboratory in order to participate. Theoretically I suppose they could,[3] but population-based experiments are infinitely more practical when the representative samples are not required to show up in a single location.

To clarify further, for purposes of this volume, when I use the term "experiment" in the context of population-based survey experiments, I am referring to studies in which the researcher controls the random assignment of participants to variations of the independent variable in order to observe their effects on a dependent variable. Importantly, the term "experiment" is often used far more broadly than this particular definition. For example, many classic "experiments" such as Galileo's observation of gravitational acceleration do not involve random assignment to conditions. And in the social sciences, Milgram's famous demonstration of obedience to authority initially lacked any second group or source of comparison, although he later added these to his design.

---

[2] I use the terms "population-based survey experiment" and "population-based experiment" interchangeably throughout.

[3] The efforts closest to attempting this are studies of deliberative democracy that bring random samples of citizens together for face to face discussion (see Warren and Pearse 2008; Ackerman and Fishkin, 2004).

So while there are many important experiments that do not meet this definition, I exclude these types of studies from my definition of population-based survey experiments for two reasons. First, in order to be able to make clear statements about the contribution of population-based experiments to internal and external validity, I must limit discussion to experiments for which these two ends are indeed primary goals. Establishing causality and generalizing to a defined target population are not always the goals of research, but they are central to the majority of social scientific work. In addition, the type of experimentation I circumscribe is where population-based survey experiments have the most to offer. Other kinds of experimental studies undoubtedly could benefit from more diverse subject populations as well, but given that experiments that fall outside of this definition are focused on other purposes, this methodological development is less important to these types of studies. However, when scholars want to be certain that a given relationship involves cause and effect, and that their theory may be generalized beyond a narrow pool of subjects, then this is precisely the context in which population-based survey experiments can make their biggest contribution.

Strictly speaking, population-based survey experiments are more experiment than survey. By design, population-based experiments are experimental studies drawing on the power of random assignment to establish unbiased causal inferences. They are also administered to randomly selected, representative samples of the target population of interest, just as a survey would be. However, population-based experiments need not (and often have not) relied on nationally representative population samples. The population of interest might be members of a particular ethnic group, parents of children under the age of 18, those who watch television news, or some other group, but the key is that convenience samples are abandoned in favor of samples representing the target population of interest.

The advantage of population-based survey experiments is that theories can be tested on samples that are representative of the populations to which they are said to apply. The downside of this trade-off is that most researchers have little experience in administering experimental treatments outside of a laboratory setting, so new techniques and considerations come into play, as described at length in this volume.

WHY NOW?

In one sense, population-based survey experiments are not new at all; simplified versions of them have been around at least since the early years of survey research in the United States. However, technological developments in survey research, combined with the development of innovative techniques in experimental design, have made highly complex and methodologically sophisticated population-based experiments increasingly accessible to social scientists across many disciplines. Unfortunately, aside from a few journal articles that have been contributed by early adopters of this technique,[4] there has been no book to date addressing this topic in a comprehensive and accessible fashion.

Population-based experiments are neither fish nor fowl. As a result, the guidelines available in textbooks for each of these individual methods—for example, the considerations related to internal and external validity, the design advice, and so forth—do not address concerns specific to population-based experiments. The purpose of this volume is to fill this niche, and thus to encourage wider and more informed use of this technique across the social sciences.

Why is the population-based experimental approach emerging as a distinct methodological option only now? Two technological innovations have brought about the emergence of this method. The first was the development of technology for computer-assisted telephone interviewing (CATI). Until the development of CATI, there were rigid constraints on experimental designs executed in the context of large population samples. The classic "split-ballot" experiment allowed for variation of a single facet, whereas current technologies allow for multiple variations of multiple factors. It has become unnecessary to produce many different versions of a paper questionnaire because the software simply does this for you, with the appropriate variation of the experimental stimulus automatically popping up on the interviewer's computer screen. This advance has allowed researchers to execute extremely complex experimental designs on large and diverse subject pools via telephone surveys.

In addition, the development of the Internet has further expanded the possibilities for population-based experiments. Although Internet-based interviewing of representative population samples is still in its infancy at this point, it is already possible to provide pictorial stimuli as well as video footage to random samples of respondents. The ability to exploit such dynamic data collection instruments has expanded the methodological repertoire and the inferential range of social scientists in many fields. Although population-based survey experiments were done by telephone or face to face long before Internet-based interviewing emerged, the Internet has greatly increased their potential.

The many advances in interviewing technology present social science with the potential to introduce some of its most important hypotheses to virtual laboratories scattered nationwide. Whether they are evaluating theoretical hypotheses, examining the robustness of laboratory findings, or

---

[4] See Piazza, Sniderman, and Tetlock (1989).

testing empirical hypotheses of other varieties, scientists' abilities to experiment on large and diverse subject pools now enable them to address important social and behavioral phenomena with greater effectiveness and efficiency.

WHO USES POPULATION-BASED EXPERIMENTS?

Population-based experiments can and have been used by social scientists in sociology, political science, psychology, economics, cognitive science, law, public health, communication, and public policy, to name just a few of the major fields that find this approach appealing. But the list does not end there. Population-based experiments have been utilized in more than twenty disciplines including psychiatry, anthropology, business, demography, African American studies, medicine, computer science, Middle Eastern studies, education, history, and even aviation studies. So long as the perceptions, behaviors, or attitudes of human beings are of interest, and the researcher's goal is to test a causal proposition of some kind, population-based survey experiments are likely to be valuable. But they are particularly so when the study is one that would benefit from combining the internal validity of experiments with the external validity of representative population samples.

My personal interest in population-based experiments stems in part from my experiences as an avid user of this method in my own research. In graduate school I was nominally trained in both survey and experimental methods, but these were conceived of as alternative rather than synthesizable approaches. The extent to which experiments were integrated with survey work was limited to tests of alternative question wording, the kind of study that was focused on minor methodological advances rather than substantively focused survey or experimental research. Given that I was not particularly interested in survey measurement issues, this did not seem like an exciting approach to me at the time. But just a few years later, I became aware of the potential this method offered for examining substantive research hypotheses and began incorporating it regularly into my own research.

Beginning in 2001, Arthur (Skip) Lupia and I served as the original principal investigators involved in Time-sharing Experiments for the Social Sciences (TESS), a large-scale infrastructure project supported by the National Science Foundation which had as its mission to promote methodological innovation through the use of population-based survey experiments. Our inspiration for this program came from its intellectual forerunner, The Multi-Investigator Study, which was spearheaded by Paul Sniderman of Stanford University. Paul originally gathered a group of scholars within the field of political science to share time on a single telephone survey. Each team of investigators was allotted a small amount of time on the survey, and all shared the core demographic questions. The theme that tied these studies together was methodological rather than substantive. Individually, the studies would make contributions to their respective fields and subfields. But collectively, by all using experimental designs, they would demonstrate novel ways to establish causality within the context of diverse population samples.

Skip Lupia and I were fortunate to be two of the young scholars who were invited to put experiments on the Multi-Investigator Study. This platform gave us an opportunity to test our hypotheses in a new experimental context and advanced our research agendas substantially. This relatively simple, but powerful idea demonstrated the tremendous benefits of combining separately conceived and jointly implemented original studies. There were efficiencies of both time and money in this combined effort that meant that more researchers could engage in original data collection. TESS took this idea a step further by establishing an ongoing cross-disciplinary platform for research employing population-based survey experiments.

Our desire to provide this opportunity to social science writ large was the origin of the plan for Time-sharing Experiments for the Social Sciences. Population-based survey experiments could be found here and there across the social sciences even before its inception in 2001, but with TESS, we took the spirit and success of the Multi-Investigator Studies and extended them to serve a greater number of researchers across a larger number of disciplines on an ongoing basis.

The advantages of TESS are straightforward from the perspective of users: it requires a minimum investment of investigators' time to propose a study, provides a quick turnaround time, and is free of charge as a result of generous support from the National Science Foundation. Under these circumstances, few social scientists find reason to complain. In addition, there are broader benefits that accrue from the population-based experimental approach, which I outline in greater length later in this book.

As of 2009, TESS is under the able leadership of psychologist Penny Visser of the University of Chicago, and sociologist Jeremy Freese of Northwestern University. It continues to offer graduate students and faculty from all over the world opportunities to run population-based experiments free of charge. Based on a simple streamlined online application process, proposals are reviewed within their respective disciplines, and once accepted they are placed on a data collection platform for execution on the population of interest. For details, interested researchers should visit the website, ExperimentCentral.org, where the short application (maximum of five double-spaced pages!) and review process are explained.

Indeed, the bulk of the examples I draw on in this book come from TESS-sponsored studies. By adding greater flexibility to the instruments, and establishing a streamlined review process for proposals, we were able to serve an even greater number of scholars at a lower cost per experiment. Further, by expanding TESS outside of political science, we drew on the creativity and ingenuity of a much larger pool of scholars and a much broader range of research subjects. It is this insight that added so much to our own ideas about the breadth of potential applications for population-based experiments.

In its original incarnation, TESS ran many telephone-administered population-based survey experiments, studies in which researchers administered experimental treatments aurally. However, in more recent years, Internet-based experiments have become increasingly popular for a number of reasons. Most importantly, it became possible to acquire representative samples of the U.S. population through a company that recruited via random digit dialing, but then put equipment into the homes of selected participants who were not already online, thus facilitating random probability samples that were accessible via Internet.[5] Demographic and other background information was collected in advance, thus making the required interview time per study quite short.[6]

In addition, Internet-based interviews open up possibilities for graphics, photographs, and video as part of the experimental treatments. Scholars interested in utilizing less obtrusive treatments, particularly when studying sensitive topics, found this advantage particularly desirable. Moreover, because online survey research companies have ongoing relationships with their panel participants rather than one-time encounters, it was also possible to provide monetary incentives that respondents knew they would, in fact, receive. Both telephone and Internet platforms allow the computer to assist in the interviewing procedure so that even highly complex experimental designs can be administered seamlessly.

---

[5] The survey company originally known as Intersurvey of Menlo Park, CA, but now doing business as Knowledge Networks, was the first and, to my knowledge, remains the only survey firm offering this possibility. In addition, other companies have used elaborate matching techniques to create demographically representative opt-in samples of people who were already online.

[6] TESS relied on three different survey organizations while Lupia and I served as co-PIs. For telephone surveys, the Indiana University Center for Survey Research collected national survey data for a large number of TESS participants. Knowledge Networks of Menlo Park, CA, provided access to their Internet panel sample solicited initially through random digit dialing, and then interviewed regularly via Internet using personal computers or WebTV equipment (put in the homes of those without Internet access). YouGovPolimetrix of Palo Alto, CA, also executed a few TESS studies using novel instrumentation combined with a matched sample of opt-in participants. For a discussion of the quality of these kinds of samples, see Chang and Krosnick (2009) and Yeager et al. (2009).

Chapter One

Drawing on the Advantages of Both Experiments and Surveys

Although most social scientists recognize the tremendous benefits of experimentation, the traditional laboratory context is not suitable for all important research questions, and experiments have always been more popular in some social science fields than in others. To a large extent, the emphasis on experimental versus survey methods reflects a field's emphasis on internal versus external validity, with fields such as psychology more oriented toward the former, and fields such as political science and sociology more oriented toward the latter.

Regardless of field or the emphasis of one's methodological training to date, population-based survey experiments challenge us to expand our methodological repertoire, and to reconsider the "truisms" about more traditional methods as well. For some researchers, survey methods are their primary means of data collection. There are, however, often substantial obstacles to drawing strong causal inferences from conventional survey data. Over the years, many have hoped that advances in statistical methods would allow scholars to use survey data to control for all plausible rival interpretations of a potentially causal relationship. But despite massive and impressive advances in statistical methods over the years, few people are as optimistic today that statistics can solve all of our causal inference problems. For survey researchers, population-based experiments provide a means of establishing causality that is unmatched by any large-scale survey data collection effort, no matter how extensive.

Experimentalists come to population-based experiments with a different monkey on their backs. Having solved the problem of causation in many areas of research by relying primarily, if not exclusively, on experiments, fields like psychology are commonly accused of ignoring external validity. Can we really just assume that the way that college sophomores work is the way all people work? Psychologists have made some good arguments for the generalizability of findings in areas such as basic human perceptual processes. But they are less convincing when it comes to many other areas of knowledge where generational differences or life experiences come into play.[7]

---

[7] There are some cases in which effects can be effectively extrapolated from a convenience sample to the general population. For example, as Druckman and Kam (forthcoming) note, when the treatment effect is entirely homogeneous across people, extrapolation is obviously valid. But this is a very big "if" because any dimension along which the subject population differs from the general population could potentially invalidate extrapolation. Moreover, establishing homogeneity of effects is not something we can do easily or with any certainty.

Druckman and Kam also suggest some ways to tease out the average effect in the general population from a convenience sample in cases where the treatment effect is not homogeneous. The problem with extrapolation in this case is that one must assume 1) that all rel-

In an ideal world, researchers would not be identified by method, and we would all be well-versed in a variety of approaches. But given that we are clearly not there yet, what is new and challenging about population-based experiments will vary for researchers from different fields. For this reason, I will risk redundancy at times in reviewing some basics so as not to assume too much from any particular reader. My goal in this book is not to provide a resource for the basics of experimental design, nor to discuss the fine points of survey research methods, mainly because there are much better sources on both of these topics. Instead, my goal is to stimulate the use of this approach by providing a sense of its potential and by situating population-based survey experiments in relation to experimental research and survey research. In order to accomplish these goals, it is sometimes necessary to review some basics, and I ask for the reader's forbearance in those cases.

Throughout the natural and social sciences, researchers employ experimental designs in order to combat the challenges posed by the fundamental problem of causal inference. To review the problem in a nutshell, in order for one variable to be said to "cause" another, three conditions generally must be met, the "holy trinity" of causality: (1) the two must co-vary, whether over time or across units of analysis; (2) the cause must precede the effect in time; and (3) the relationship between the cause and effect must not be explainable through some other third variable, which would render the association spurious. In practice, few scholars have problems establishing the first criterion, and the second is problematic only for studies based on cross-sectional observations in which a plausible causal argument can be made for reverse causation.

Thus the "third variable problem" is the key reason experiments are known as the gold standard for inferring causality. Experiments are the best possible way to address the problem of third variables and potentially spurious relationships. This "holy trinity" of causation is well known across the social sciences, but the third variable problem has distinguished itself because of the lack of solid approaches to resolving it. For temporal precedence, researchers can use time series designs, but there is no parallel solution to the third variable problem. In observational research, omitted variable bias plagues or at least menacingly threatens most causal arguments, and there is no simple solution short of an experimental design.[8]

---

evant moderating variables are known, that is, all possible sources of heterogeneity of effects; 2) that the general population averages for all variables that moderate the impact of treatment are also known; and 3) that measurement of the moderating variable is error-free.

[8] Over-time panel designs come the closest, but in addition to possible problems from attrition and conditioning, panels are expensive and thus few and far between.

Across the social sciences, experimental design strategies entail one of two approaches to the problem of causal inference. Researchers either (1) evaluate a unit of analysis before and after a given treatment relative to those evaluated before and after without treatment, and then draw inferences from these pre-post within-subject comparisons; or (2) use a between-group design in which different subjects are randomly assigned to groups that receive different experimental treatments, often including a control condition.[9]

What is notable is that either of these approaches, as well as far more complex experimental designs, is easily implemented in the context of surveys utilizing computer-assisted telephone interviewing platforms or Internet-based interviews. The ability to make strong causal inferences has little to do with the laboratory setting per se, and a lot to do with the ability to control the random assignment of people to different experimental treatments. By moving the possibilities for experimentation outside of the laboratory in this way, population-based experiments strengthen the internal validity of social science research and provide the potential to interest a much broader group of social scientists in the possibilities of experimentation. Of course, the fact that it *can* be done outside the lab is not a good reason in itself to do so. Thus, below I review some of the key advantages of population-based experiments, beginning with four advantages they have over traditional laboratory experiments, then ending with some of their more general benefits for the accumulation of useful social scientific knowledge.

Population Samples Rather Than Subject Pools

Most laboratory experiments rely on undergraduate subject pools created explicitly for the purpose of providing an ongoing supply of experimental subjects for researchers in one or multiple disciplines. With population-based survey experiments, scholars instead expose randomly-selected respondents to randomly-assigned treatments. A key advantage of this approach is that using survey sampling techniques, researchers can assign both *larger* and *more diverse* samples to experimental conditions of their choosing.

Anyone who has ever executed a laboratory experiment knows that it takes a lot of time, sometimes money, and often other forms of coaxing to encourage large numbers of people to show up in a laboratory at an appointed time. The easiest approach—the subject pool in which students are required to participate in some fashion—has its drawbacks in terms of sheer numbers, as well as the diversity of experimental subjects. In ad-

[9] Holland (1986, p. 947).

dition, participants in subject pools typically participate in more than one experimental study, thus making them less naïve than one might hope. By contrast, sample surveys regularly include two to three thousand people per study, and population-based survey experiments can do the same. The greater statistical power that comes with large samples makes it possible to identify more subtle differences between experimental groups.

Larger samples also make it easier to identify moderating relationships—that is, situations in which a given experimental effect is not present, or at least not equally so, across different subgroups of the population. Seldom do social science theories serve as true universals. For this reason, it is useful to know precisely what the boundaries are for a given theoretical generalization. For example, one recent population-based survey experiment established that the characteristics that make people more or less attractive to others appear not to be the same for men and women and for blacks and whites in America.[10]

In addition to sheer numbers of participants, population-based experiments also make possible broader, more diverse subject pools. Though not all social scientists require large and diverse subject populations to accomplish their research goals, many can benefit from them. Critics over the years have often questioned the extent to which the usual subjects in social science experiments resemble broader, more diverse populations. As Carl Hovland famously put it, "College sophomores may not be people."[11] Population-based survey experiments offer a powerful means for researchers to respond to such critiques, one that researchers in fields that traditionally emphasize internal validity and experimental methods will find quite useful.

For example, to study the impact of gender on worker performance evaluations, Rashotte and Webster designed an experiment in which participants were presented with a picture of a male or female individual, David or Diane. The photos were taken from a public website, www.hotornot .com, where, for inexplicable reasons, people post their pictures to be rated by anonymous others. Using these photos allowed the researchers to control for attractiveness effects, by selecting those who were rated as average. Respondents were asked about how intelligent they perceived the person to be, and how capable, along with many other characteristics.

Using this framework with college student samples, Rashotte and Webster had found small but consistent differences in evaluations of David/

[10] See Conley and Glauber (2005) and Conley (2006) for a summary. Unfortunately, most studies of attractiveness to date have used undergraduate student samples, business school graduates, or those who selected into dating services, all of which makes it difficult to identify "universal" characteristics.
[11] Attributed to Tolman, in Hovland (1959, p. 10). See also, e.g., Sears (1986).

Diane among both men and women.[12] Both groups gave higher ratings to David than Diane, regardless of whether they stated beliefs in gender equality or not. The authors concluded that these gender stereotypes operate below the radar such that both men and women expect greater competence from men.

But whether the effects exist in the population as a whole depends on whether the results for college students can be generalized to an older population, and whether the judgments the students made of other young men and women would hold if the targets were older men and women as well. Some have suggested that gender is losing its status significance over time, especially among younger generations, a claim that is difficult to address without more variance in both the targets and subjects involved in these studies.

When Rashotte and Webster replicated this same study in the general population, their findings were far less consistent by gender of target, thus calling into question the generalizability of previous findings based on student samples. Age of the target had a much stronger impact than gender did, and the findings for gender varied based on whether people were evaluating intelligence, competence, or some other dimension of status. Their results indicated that older men and women were consistently rated as more competent than younger men and women.[13]

Experimentalists can use the larger and more representative samples characteristic of population-based experiments to show that observations generated in a laboratory can be replicated under very different conditions and with far more diverse populations. If they do not replicate well, then researchers learn about the boundaries of their theories, which is also useful to the progress of scientific knowledge.

The Real World Over the Laboratory

Rightly or wrongly, evidence from population-based survey experiments is likely to be viewed by external audiences as more convincing than evidence from laboratory studies. No one disputes that laboratory experiments provide strong tests of causal propositions, but scientific and popular audiences often want more than evidence of causality. In many cases, observers want a demonstration that laboratory observations survive exposure to myriad conditions outside of the lab. For example, the laboratory setting is often assumed to make people act more responsibly than would otherwise be the case without the close supervision of the experimenter. People know when they are being watched, and may act differently as a result. In

---

[12] Rashotte and Webster (2005a).
[13] Rashotte and Webster (2005b).

addition, the distractions of everyday life can reduce the likelihood that a treatment will have an impact; if an effect can only be obtained when unrealistically high levels of attention are directed toward a stimulus, then the effect probably does not occur as often in the real world.

As I emphasize in Chapter 8, too much importance is routinely attributed to laboratory versus field settings, when other factors probably play a much more important role in external validity. However, this is not to say that settings are completely irrelevant. The importance of situational influences on human behavior is clear and well-documented;[14] despite our tendency to think otherwise, the same people will behave very differently under different circumstances. But this fact aptly illustrates the oversimplification surrounding the idea that conducting research in "the field" means it will easily generalize elsewhere. One field setting may be nothing like another, despite the fact that both are outside the lab.

Research Designed Around Specific Subpopulations

Yet another advantage that population-based experiments provide over laboratory experiments is the ability to study specialized subpopulations. Particularly when utilizing respondents from ongoing Internet panels, investigators typically know a great deal about their experimental subjects in advance. These respondents are generally "prescreened" for a variety of characteristics during an initial recruitment interview, so characteristics such as race, region, income, employment status and so forth are already known. This makes it possible to sample specific subpopulations or to block respondents based on characteristics known to affect the dependent variable. Under ordinary circumstances in laboratory studies, sampling subpopulations is either massively inefficient (because large numbers of ineligible participants will need to be screened out and turned away) and/or it makes subjects too aware of exactly why they were selected, which threatens the integrity of the results. The use of ongoing panels eliminates many of these problems.

For example, using equally-sized samples of respondents who had previously identified themselves as white American, black American, or Asian American, Cottrell and Neuberg randomly assigned these three groups to evaluate one of each of these same three ethnic groups.[15] Respondents reported both general favorability toward the specific group, and a list of discrete emotions such as anger, fear, pity, envy, respect, etc. They also reported on a variety of specific kinds of threats that they perceived the randomly assigned group posed to "people like me."

---

[14] See Ross and Nisbett (1991).
[15] See Cottrell and Neuberg (2005).

The investigators found that outgroup prejudice was not all cut of the same cloth; there were distinct emotional profiles underlying sometimes identical levels of favorability (or the lack thereof) toward a group. Interestingly, in this case their population-based findings closely mirrored results from student samples, with African Americans eliciting mainly fear, pity, and anger, whereas Asian Americans generated pity and resentment, but no fear. This work highlights the fact that prejudice as traditionally conceived often masks very different emotional responses to different groups. Moreover, different groups often have qualitatively different prejudices toward the very same group. This kind of information is quite valuable to those who seek to combat prejudice and would have been far more difficult to obtain within a standard lab setting.

In addition to advantages over laboratory experiments in particular, population-based survey experiments also have some general strengths as a methodological approach. These advantages are not characteristics exclusive to this one method, but they are secondary benefits that help make a case for adding this approach to the broader collection of research tools at our disposal. More specifically, population-based survey experiments are likely to encourage more widespread use of experiments by social scientists, the use of complex experimental designs, more successive studies comprising a larger research agenda, and research that speaks to real world events and policies.

Encouraging Greater Use of Experimental Designs

Experiments play a critical role in advancing social science. Scholars have long recognized the power of experiments, acknowledging them as the best possible approach when attempting to draw causal inferences empirically. For many research questions, experiments are simply the most effective means of evaluating competing causal hypotheses. As much as we would love it if it were true, there simply are no statistical techniques for observational data that provide the power and elegance of an experimental design.

Nonetheless, there remains considerable resistance to the use of experiments in some fields, mainly because of researchers' concerns about the generalizability of research findings produced in a lab and/or with college student subjects. One advantage of population-based survey experiments is that by overcoming these restrictions, they offer the prospect of luring more social scientists into experimental research. By eliminating the most common objections to experimental work, population-based experiments promise to increase the number of scholars and the breadth of fields regularly using experimental designs.

For example, scholars can use population-based experiments to clarify the causal implications of findings from conventional surveys. Experiments often make it possible to resolve the direction of a causal relationship that has been difficult to disentangle. For example, do high levels of social trust lead people to buy products online, or does buying online lead people to have higher levels of social trust? As described further in Chapter 6, there is now experimental evidence that, in fact, both causal processes take place.

In addition to providing a means of resolving direction of causation and ruling out potentially spurious relationships, population-based experiments can help advance theory in research areas where selection bias makes observational studies relatively unproductive. For example, one puzzle in international relations involves the question of whether "audience costs" exist; that is, if one country's leaders threaten another country, are there penalties for the country's leaders if they do not follow through on their threat? Do leaders who make empty threats risk losing the faith of their constituents in addition to losing credibility with the country they have threatened?

Audience costs have long been believed to exist, but it is difficult to document them because if leaders take the *prospect* of audience costs into account when they make foreign policy decisions, then they are unlikely to back down because they believe citizens would react negatively to such a decision. So social scientists doing observational research are denied the opportunity to observe a public backlash against the leader in all but a very few cases; leaders self-select into making only threats that they are willing to back up.

What is a social scientist to do? We could attempt to persuade leaders to make idle threats and then back down just for the heck of it—or at least for the sake of gathering scientific knowledge on the price that would be paid. Unfortunately (or perhaps fortunately), such an appeal is unlikely to be successful with most national leaders, although some undoubtedly have their price. Alternatively, political scientist Michael Tomz administered a population-based experiment to a representative sample of Americans, asking each person about "a situation our country has faced many times in the past and will probably face again. Different leaders have handled the situation in different ways. We will describe one approach U.S. leaders have taken, and ask whether you approve or disapprove."[16]

Respondents were then told about a crisis in which "a country sent its military to take over a neighboring country." As the author describes:

---

[16] Tomz (2007, p. 824).

The country was led by a "dictator" in half the interviews, and a "democratically elected government" in the other half. The attacker sometimes had aggressive motives—it invaded "to get more power and resources"—and sometimes invaded "because of a long-standing historical feud." To vary power, I informed half the participants that the attacker had a "strong military," such that "it would have taken a major effort for the United States to help push them out," and told the others that the attacker had a "weak military," which the United States could have repelled without major effort. Finally, a victory by the attacking country would either "hurt" or "not affect" the safety and economy of the United States.[17]

Respondents also learned how the U.S. president had handled the situation, either (a) promising to stay out and then doing so, with the attacking country eventually taking over its neighbor; or (b) promising the help of the U.S. military to push out the invaders, but not doing so, with the attacking country taking over its neighbor. If audience costs exist, the respondents who heard that the president threatened but did not carry out his threat should approve less of his handling of the situation than those who heard that he stuck by his original decision to stay out.

Results of the study suggest that audience costs do indeed exist across the population and under broad conditions; those who heard that the president issued an empty threat were significantly more disapproving than those told he never intended to get involved. Experimental designs such as this one allow researchers to test causal hypotheses that there is no other way to empirically verify outside of historical case studies. As reviews of such experiments reveal, population-based experimental designs have already generated important discoveries in many social sciences.[18]

More Complex Experimental Designs

Population-based experiments can accommodate a large number of experimental conditions. In part, this capacity is due to the larger samples noted above. But it is not only a function of sample size. In a laboratory, an experimental design with nearly 100 different experimental conditions would be considered insane to attempt unless the treatments were administered by computer. But in population-based experiments, such numbers are not uncommon precisely because a computer program determines the

---

[17] Tomz (2007).
[18] Sniderman and Grob (1996).

treatment a given respondent receives, whether it is administered online or via telephone interview.[19]

For example, Sniderman, Piazza, Tetlock, and Kendrick used a population-based experiment to see whether combinations of individual characteristics combined with race would trigger respondents to be less likely to help black rather than white victims of unemployment.[20] Their laid-off worker experiment varied descriptions of the unemployed person along six different dimensions (age, sex, race, marital and parental status, dependability) that were each manipulated orthogonal to the other, creating a total of 96 conditions. A person was described as having been "laid off because the company where they worked had to reduce its staff" and was either black or white, male or female, in their early twenties, mid-thirties, or early forties, and single, a single parent, married, or married with children, along with being (or not) a dependable worker. Respondents were next asked, "Think for a moment about each person and then tell me how much government help, if any, that person should receive while looking for a new job."[21]

Respondents then had the option of suggesting a lot of government help, some, or none at all. The many possible variations of this highly complex treatment were easily administered in the context of a population-based experiment. Further, the larger sample sizes characteristic of population-based experiments allowed sufficient statistical power to identify even fairly modest effect sizes. The sample sizes alone would have been prohibitive in allowing execution of this study in a lab. Given that the characteristics of the target person were each randomly assigned, each attribute was orthogonal to every other attribute, thus making it possible to assess the statistically independent impact of each characteristic as well as their interactions.

By facilitating more complicated experimental designs, population-based experiments allow researchers to study complex interactions. For example, in the study described above, the "new racism" thesis suggested that white respondents (and white conservatives in particular) would be especially unlikely to recommend government help for black victims of unemployment who violated social norms, either by failing to keep their family intact or by failing to be reliable workers. Such was not the case

---

[19] Although computer-administered experiments can be done in a lab setting, what would be the point of using a convenience sample in a lab, when the same study could be administered to a random sample via computer as well? Cost would seem to be the only advantage (assuming laboratory subjects are free, which is not always the case).

[20] Sniderman et al. (1991).

[21] Sniderman et al. (1991, p. 427).

according to their results, but without a complex factorial design, it would have been difficult to test this hypothesis.

Facilitating Research Agendas

Relative to traditional surveys, population-based experiments are well suited to take advantage of sequential data collection efforts, mainly because this approach tends to be driven to a greater extent by the desire to test specific hypotheses and because it requires the collection of a relatively small number of variables. As with any experiment, the whole point of a population-based experiment is typically to evaluate a specific hypothesis or a small set of hypotheses. By contrast, much (although certainly not all) non-experimental survey design seeks to collect all the data the researcher can think of (or afford) bearing on a particular issue, and then see what emerges as important later in the analysis. Survey analyses are observational rather than experimental, so a large number of questions must be asked in order to rule out potentially spurious relationships. Because opportunities for survey data collection are limited and may be restricted to just one large effort, survey researchers must anticipate in advance all possible variables needed for many possible hypotheses, and then put them together in one survey.

This characterization is not a critique of survey research or of survey researchers. While it is tempting to think that whatever additions or refinements that could be made on a subsequent survey could have been done on the first survey if the researcher had just thought long enough and hard enough, this is simply not how social science (or natural science, for that matter) progresses. Often the hypotheses that form the basis for the second data collection depend upon what was learned from the first data collection. But given that relatively few social scientists have even one such opportunity for original data collection, still fewer benefit from successive studies of the same topic. Survey research generally *must* be of an omnibus nature due to the need to include potentially spurious "third variables," and the need for a larger sample size due to statistical issues.

Successive population-based survey experiments tend to be more self-contained. The experimental design means that the study requires a much smaller number of questions than an observational study testing the same hypothesis. In addition, the use of simpler statistical models means that one can often get by with a smaller sample size. The treatments are designed to test particular hypotheses, rather than dozens and dozens of potential hypotheses. As a result of the more focused quality of experiments, they tend to be smaller and less expensive, thereby conserving resources. Resources can be put toward subsequent studies that build on what was learned in the first. For these reasons, population-based experiments are well suited to the gradual, systematic accumulation of knowledge.

Research that Speaks to Real World Events and Policies

Population-based experiments are ideal for taking advantage of quickly unfolding opportunities for experiments embedded in real world events. So-called "firehouse studies" that are executed quickly in response to naturally occurring and often unpredictable events are facilitated by the existence of infrastructure to sample and contact respondents. In the past, opportunities for studies of this kind were scarce because of the substantial lead time needed to contact appropriate samples and get studies into the field. Because Internet-based survey panels have already established contact with potential participants and often have gathered extensive demographics in advance as well, it is possible to contact a large number of respondents quickly as events arise that researchers wish to study.

For example, in the midst of the 2004 controversy over the Georgia state flag, which still featured the Confederate battle emblem at the time, Hutchings and Walton did a population-based experiment focused strictly on residents of the state of Georgia using a blocked design such that half of the respondents were black and half were white.[22] A number of other population-based experiments were designed around real world events such as Hurricane Katrina, which ravaged New Orleans in 2005, as well as the role of partisanship in attributions of blame for the terrorist attacks of 9/11.[23] In short, population-based survey experiments make it easier to jump on real world events that present unique research opportunities.

In addition to event-based studies, population-based survey experiments also offer advantages for studies designed specifically to inform public policy. Take, for example, the study described at greater length in Chapter 3, which examined how much extra money per month people would be willing to pay for health insurance that includes new vaccines for themselves and their children—vaccines that otherwise must be covered out of pocket.[24] The answer to this research question is obviously relevant to the design of healthcare options to maximize public health.

But assuming a study is designed to answer this question, what kind of study would maximize its policy impact? The answer becomes clear after considering the more traditional options for empirical research, surveys,

---

[22] Hutchings, Walton, and Benjamin (2005).

[23] For example, Huber, Van Boven, Park, and Pizzi (2006, 2007); Shaker and Ben-Porath (2010); Malhotra and Kuo (2008, 2009); Willer and Adams (2008).

[24] See Davis and Fant (2005) or Chapter 3 of this volume.

and experiments. Would a survey simply asking a representative sample of people how much they would pay for this benefit produce a convincing course of action? Possibly, but given that most people have no idea up front how much vaccines should cost, their answers are likely to be all over the map. Perhaps more importantly, using a traditional experiment, would policymakers really be swayed to alter the structure of health care options by evidence based on a sample of college students, most of whom do not have children and have never purchased health insurance or paid premiums through their place of employment? This seems highly unlikely. But by conducting an experimental study with a representative sample of parents, researchers are able to provide policymakers with greater confidence in the findings while also enhancing the relevance of their research to real world policy questions.

OVERVIEW

In this introductory chapter, I have outlined the development of population-based experiments and highlighted some of their advantages over traditional experiments and surveys. In the remainder of the book, I make the case for this method as a unique contribution to social science methodology, and provide extensive examples of how it has been used thus far. I also discuss some of the problems that are common to population-based survey experiments, and suggest best practices for future users.

There is a tendency to think about population-based survey experiments as simply a hybrid methodology that melds certain characteristics of surveys and experiments. But to say this tells us nothing about *which* advantages and disadvantages of each methodology are inherited. As I further argue in the concluding chapter, population-based experiments are not simply a mix of two methods in the sense that quasi-experimental designs are a hybrid of observational and experimental techniques.[25] Instead they are more akin to an agricultural hybrid that produces something that was not present in either of the two original plants. To the extent that population-based survey experiments can be implemented with effective treatments and with the same degree of control over random assignment as in the lab, it is the only kind of research design capable of simply and straightforwardly estimating population average treatment effects without complex statistical machinations. This characteristic makes population-based experiments unique. They are not without their limitations, to be

---

[25] For example, some suggest that quasi-experiments inherit the weaknesses of both experiments and field studies (Marsh, 1982).

sure, but those limitations do not lie in our ability to draw important conclusions from them so much as in our ability to execute this method well.

Toward that end, Part I of the book focuses on the greatest challenge facing population-based experiments—how to implement effective treatments outside the laboratory via remote communication technologies. I provide an overview of many different kinds of population-based experiments, drawing on the wealth of creativity provided by TESS participants as well as other researchers. These designs are by no means the only or necessarily the best possible ways to execute population-based experiments. But I provide this sample template of designs as a means of stimulating readers' own creativity as to the possibilities that population-based experiments offer their field of research. In Chapter 2, I describe population-based experiments designed to improve measurement. These are descendants of the early split-ballot approach, also geared toward improving measurement of attitudes and behaviors, but the approaches are now far more sophisticated and complex. In Chapter 3, I describe direct and indirect treatments, that is, treatments that either directly and overtly try to move the respondent in a particular direction, or that indirectly do so in a more unobtrusive (and often clever) manner. Chapters 4 and 5 cover two approaches to implementing highly complex population-based experimental treatments: vignette treatments and game-based treatments, respectively. Vignettes offer the possibility of easily executing complex, multi-dimensional factorial designs. Game-based treatments are an outgrowth of conducting experiments online, where gaming seems only natural, and where highly complex, multi-stage experimental treatments can be experienced by participants. Ideally, Part I of the book should serve as an organizational framework and as an idea generator, helping those in one discipline see the promise of what has been pilot-tested already in another.

In Part II, I address a series of practical matters in the design and implementation of population-based survey experiments. The TESS staff benefited from its involvement in hundreds of different population-based experiments, and we learned a lot from these experiences. In Chapter 6, I try to eliminate the need for others to learn by trial and error as we did. Hopefully some of our errors will allow others to avoid wasting time and money by falling prey to the same problems. The practical issues addressed range from "How do I explain a population-based experiment to my Institutional Review Board (IRB)?" to "What can I do to maximize the effectiveness of a treatment in a population-based experiment?" to "How should I think about measurement differently from when I am designing a survey?" Not surprisingly, different disciplines had different problems adapting to the idea of a population-based experiment, and I use various war stories from TESS to illustrate the kinds of problems most likely to plague users from different disciplines.

In Chapter 7, I address three common problems that emerge in the analysis stage. These include the misguided practice of doing randomization checks, whether and how to use survey weights, and the use and misuse of covariates. Finally, in Chapters 8 and 9, I situate this approach within the broader arsenal of social scientific tools. To understand the methodological contribution of population-based survey experiments, it is important to understand what they do and do not accomplish relative to more widely examined methods such as laboratory experiments and surveys. The common argument in their favor—that they boost generalizability—is a bit overly simplistic. To understand why, Chapter 8 takes a serious look at what generalizability really means. Experimentalists often go to great lengths to argue that student or other convenience samples are not problematic in terms of external validity. These arguments are sometimes convincing, and sometimes not.[26] Likewise, a convincing case for causality is often elusive with observational research, no matter how stridently one might argue to the contrary.

As students of the social sciences learn early on, the conventional wisdom is that experiments are widely valued for their internal validity, and experiments lack external validity. These assumptions are so widespread as to go without question in most disciplines, particularly those emphasizing external validity, such as political science and sociology. In disciplines where the experimental method dominates, such as psychology, experiments are viewed with less suspicion. But observational studies, such as surveys, are still supposed to be better for purposes of maximizing external validity because this method allows studying people in real world settings.

Strangely enough given our vocation as social scientists, most of us—myself included—accepted these truisms without benefit of conceptual elaboration or empirical evidence. Upon reconsideration, I suggest that the internal and external validity of any given study has at best very little to do with whether it was done in a laboratory or a field setting. Random assignment, rather than any particular setting, is what allows for strong claims about internal validity. Likewise, there is no logical or empirical basis for claiming the inherent superiority of one research setting over another for purposes of external validity. For this reason, I argue that a different approach to assessing the generalizability of studies is needed. This approach allows us to more accurately situate the contributions of population-based survey experiments in the existing collection of methodological tools.

---

[26] For a discussion of issues surrounding the use of student subjects, see Druckman and Kam (2010).

PART I

TREATMENTS FOR POPULATION-BASED
EXPERIMENTAL DESIGNS

Treatments to Improve Measurement

THE GOAL OF PART I of this volume is to supply numerous examples of different types of population-based experimental treatments from a variety of different social science fields. Chapter 2 begins where population-based experiments commenced, with experimental studies designed to improve measurement of concepts and behaviors that are difficult to quantify accurately. The additional chapters in Part I are organized around five loosely defined categories of treatment, any of which could be put to use to answer research questions in any discipline.

Chapter 3 describes the most straightforward and transparent of treatment varieties, the direct treatment, as well as progressively more subtle and unobtrusive interventions, dubbed indirect treatments. Chapters 4 and 5 explore two techniques that are particularly well suited to highly complex experiments: vignette treatments and treatments encapsulated within the context of games.

In some cases, multiple treatment classifications can be envisioned for a given approach, so these are to be understood simply as working categories, distinctions that are, in some cases, unclear. For researchers looking for design ideas, which category a given approach to treatment falls into is unimportant; the classification scheme serves mainly to allow readers to get a sense of the broad range of possibilities offered by population-based experiments.

The experimental treatments discussed in this chapter are not designed to test a specific theoretical hypothesis so much as to improve measurement. Although I generally make a distinction between testing hypotheses and improving measurement, in many cases the fundamental hypothesis of a study is that a measure is flawed in some systematic way. So at times these two purposes—improving measurement and testing hypotheses—are indeed one and the same. If my hypothesis is that white people are not completely honest in self-reporting their personal views about minority groups, then I am also hypothesizing that social desirability is skewing the measurement of whites' perceptions of minority groups. And if I hypothesize that people will systematically over-report their exposure to news about politics and public affairs because it is a socially desirable behavior, I cannot test this without implicitly also investigating how to improve measurement of this construct.

To date, three general approaches to improving measurement are evident in population-based experiments. I begin by discussing the "item count technique" or "list experiment," which is especially appropriate when a socially desirable or undesirable judgment is being assessed. Second, I discuss a variety of strategies that involve altering the inferential process used in coming up with answers to questions. In the third section I focus on techniques involving anchoring as a means of improving measurement. These are undoubtedly not the only approaches that can be undertaken, but they convey a sense of the possibilities.

Survey researchers are not naïve about their ability to capture attitudes and behaviors validly and reliably. They have long known that survey questions can be sensitive and unpredictable in the systematic influences they may exercise. In fact, early population-based experiments were in the service of improving survey measurement techniques rather than executing experiments for their own sake. The so-called "split-ballot technique" allowed survey researchers to randomly assign respondents to one of two versions of a given survey, typically in order to determine if modified question wording made a systematic difference in the answers that were given. Quite often it did.

Scholars have used population-based experiments for similar purposes, drawing more specifically on techniques that hold the promise of decreasing false but socially desirable responses, or of increasing true but socially undesirable responses. In either case, measurement is improved. These techniques represent a departure from the traditional means that survey researchers use to guard against social desirability pressures. The more traditional approach was to try to make all possible responses equally easy to offer through the use of introductory scripts that assure respondents anonymity and stress the importance of honest answers. For example, in the case of voting, which is assumed to be socially desirable, the standard question is generally something along these lines:

> In talking to people about the election we often find that a lot of people were not able to vote because they were not registered or they were sick or they just did not have time. How about you, did you vote in the elections this November?

It is as if the interviewer is telling the respondent, "Really, it is ok, there are lots of good reasons not to vote." On the other hand, when tapping a socially *undesirable* behavior, such as tax evasion, the concern is with false negatives rather than false positives, so researchers tend to bend over backwards to assure people of anonymity and encourage affirmative responses.

Because many are convinced that people will still not admit to some attitudes and behaviors, another approach is asking people how likely it is that *other* people, or perhaps their neighbors, engage in some socially undesirable behavior such as cheating on one's taxes. While it is possible that people project their own views onto others even when they will not admit it themselves, it is difficult for researchers to support this assertion with hard evidence. Moreover, as the results of novel population-based experiments have demonstrated, such techniques—whether they are assurances of anonymity, readily available excuses for lack of socially desirable answers, or something else—may not be enough to eliminate all pressures. The need to ask questions about attitudes and behaviors that are fraught with social baggage means that researchers have had to come up with innovative new approaches to these problems, and population-based experiments are an ideal solution.

Population-based experiments are especially useful for improving measurement when researchers have accurate aggregate-level estimates of some behavior among a given population, such as the nation as a whole. These estimates can then be used to verify which survey measurement technique is most accurate. For example, there are widely available statistics on what percentage of the population votes in national elections and how many people tune into a given television program. All survey research can benefit from knowing the extent that one measurement technique comes closer than another to some standard of accuracy.

In many cases, we are well aware that a measure is not valid, but we do not know exactly why, nor what to do about it. Given that experiments and surveys both rely heavily on self-reports, it is difficult to underestimate the importance of improving measurement. It is easy to get less excited about methodological and measurement-oriented population-based experiments relative to substantive ones, but their respective levels of pizzazz bear little relation to the importance of their contributions to knowledge.

THE LIST TREATMENT OR ITEM COUNT TECHNIQUE

List treatments are designed to allow the endorsement of sensitive or controversial positions and behaviors without requiring the respondent to directly admit to them. Instead of openly endorsing a given attitude or admitting to a particular behavior, the respondent answers indirectly by reporting the number of items that are applicable to him from a list of several activities. One of the items, the target, is on the list for only a randomly selected half of the sample. So, for example, when assessing attitudes toward race, respondents were randomly assigned to two groups who were read these instructions:

> Now I am going to read you [three/four] things that sometimes make people angry or upset. After I read all [three/four], just tell me HOW MANY of them upset you. I don't want to know which ones, just HOW MANY.[1]

Both groups were read three non-sensitive items:

1. the federal government increasing the tax on gasoline
2. professional athletes getting million dollar salaries
3. large corporations polluting the environment

The baseline group was read only these three items, but respondents in the treatment group also received an additional item (known as the target item), the central attitude or behavior of interest to the researcher:

4. a black family moving in next door

After reading the list, the interviewer in the telephone survey then asked, "How many of these [three/four] make you angry or upset?" and recorded the number offered by the respondent. The respondent was not required to reveal to the interviewer which items, only the total number. Thus, by comparing to the control (three item) condition, the investigators could estimate the extent to which responses to the target item were deflated (or in other cases inflated) due to social desirability.

Importantly, based on these responses, it is impossible to know the answer to the target item for any given individual. But the difference between the mean number of items chosen in the treatment group and the control group can be attributed to either sampling error or the presence of the fourth item. By subtracting these means and multiplying by 100, the researcher constructs an estimate of the percentage of respondents opposed to the sensitive item.

In this particular study, the investigators found evidence of significant suppression of anti-black racial attitudes using traditional direct questions. Most interestingly, the unobtrusive, list-based estimates suggested that the "New South" thesis, the idea that the South is no longer any different in racial attitudes than the rest of the country, is simply not true. Using the unobtrusive measures, racial prejudice in the South was sig-

---

[1] This example comes from Kuklinski, Cobb, and Gilens (1997, p. 323–49).

nificantly greater than in other areas of the country, and particularly so among Southern men.

When the contaminating effects of social desirability are eliminated, many social scientific findings turn out to be quite different from what we had thought. For example, traditional polls suggest that only 5 to 15 percent of Americans say they will not vote for a female presidential candidate, and yet the list technique suggests that roughly 26 percent of the population gets "angry or upset" about "a woman serving as president."[2] This same technique has been used to derive more accurate assessments on sensitive topics involving race,[3] religion,[4] and homosexuality,[5] to name just a few examples. List-based results also suggest a higher percentage of shoplifters in the general population relative to a direct survey question, particularly among females, the middle-aged, and well-educated respondents.[6]

Concerns about social desirability bias tend to be greatest when asking about sensitive and socially undesirable topics, so this is naturally where list experiments have been put to greatest use. However, they can as easily be applied to situations in which people over-report positive behaviors as well. For as long as I can remember, political polls in the United States have been criticized—if not laughed at—for their tendency to vastly overestimate the percentage of Americans who turn out to vote. It has been assumed that because voting is considered by many to be a "civic duty," over-reporting simply reflects the social desirability of this behavior. In other words, people intentionally misrepresent themselves and report voting when in many cases they did not.

So can researchers reduce social desirability bias in self-reports of turnout by using a more anonymous means of assessing the behavior? A series of experimental studies by Holbrook and Krosnick was designed to answer this question.[7] Using population-based experiments embedded in telephone surveys as well as on an Internet survey platform, they successfully implemented the list technique in both contexts. Their findings suggested that the list technique significantly reduced social desirability bias and lowered estimates of self-reported voting in the telephone surveys relative to directly asking respondents this same question. However, the list technique only made a difference in the population-based experiments executed by live interviewers on the telephone with respondents.

[2] Streb, Burrell, Frederick, and Genovese (2008).
[3] Kuklinski, Cobb, and Gilens (1997); Sniderman and Carmines (1997); Gilens, Sniderman, and Kuklinski (1998).
[4] Kane, Craig, and Wald (2004).
[5] Goldman (2008).
[6] Tsuchiya, Hirai, and Ono (2007).
[7] Holbrook and Krosnick (2004).

When interviewed via Internet, without a real human being directly receiving these answers, the list technique did not lower the rate of self-reported voting relative to directly asking about it. Estimates suggested that the Internet-based interviews already reduced social desirability by eliminating the human interviewer from the process.

When the list experiment demonstrates a difference between obtrusive and unobtrusive estimates, researchers often interpret this to mean that there is social desirability associated with providing responses to this particular attitude/behavior item. But this will not be the case with every issue, nor with every interviewing technique. For example, Janus did not find a significant difference between unobtrusive and obtrusive estimates of the number of Americans supporting same-sex marriages.[8] Tsuchiya and colleagues found that, relative to direct questioning, the list technique produced higher estimates of the number of people who admitted to shoplifting by nearly 10 percentage points, while questions about blood donation were unaffected.[9]

Limitations of the List Technique

As noted above, inferences regarding whether or not people are suppressing socially undesirable characteristics or statements come strictly from the significance of the mean comparison. Although the inability to produce individual-level measures of racism, opposition to immigration, and so forth might be deemed a limitation of this approach, it is not a very serious one for most purposes.

Take, for example, a recent list experiment used to assess social desirability in people's professed beliefs in biological conceptions of race. This is a puzzling topic because on the one hand, Americans now routinely link genetics to individual behavior in casual conversations. The success of scientists who are mapping the human genome has definitely seeped into popular consciousness. On the other hand, biological understandings of racial inequality have also supposedly fallen from favor. To suggest that inequality has some genetic basis is to risk being seen as a racist. The question Brueckner and colleagues asked is whether people truly no longer believe in such explanations, or simply know better than to suggest such a thing publicly.[10] The results of their list study suggested that around 20 percent of non-blacks in the United States agree that "Genetic differences contribute to income inequality between black and white people." When asked directly, significantly fewer people endorsed this statement.

[8] Janus (2006).
[9] Tsuchiya, Hirai and Ono (2007).
[10] Brueckner, Morning, and Nelson (2005).

30

But the researchers wanted to know *what kind* of people believed in the explanatory power of genetics without admitting it. Even though list experiments cannot tell researchers which *individuals* hold a particular view, they most definitely can tell us what kinds of people are subject to social desirability influence. In this particular case, false negatives (believers who said they did not) were most pronounced among the highly educated, women, and older people. Unless one truly cared about the views of an individually identifiable respondent (a situation that should strike terror in the heart of any university's IRB), aggregated comparisons are not all that limiting for purposes of what most social scientists want to know.

Real limitations occur when investigators want to do more than bivariate analyses; multivariate analyses of list experiments reach their limits quickly due to diminishing degrees of freedom and cell sizes when crossing two or more predictors. Alternative statistical approaches that allow multivariate analyses are in development, but limitations remain.[11] Moreover, there have been relatively few studies of this technique to date, so researchers have yet to fully understand how the design can be made to work most effectively. For example, the number of non-target attitudes or behaviors in the list can affect results. And the list technique may have greater difficulty in identifying stigmatizing behaviors with generally low prevalence rates.[12] Further study may help researchers optimize list experiments for a variety of different research purposes.

IMPROVED MEASUREMENT THROUGH ALTERED INFERENCE PROCESSES

A variety of techniques have been directed toward improving measurement by altering the way people think about the question they are asked, and the process by which they come up with an answer. One effort to improve measurement involves what has been dubbed "implicit goal priming." Prior to eliciting self-reports about a socially sensitive behavior, such as excessive alcohol consumption, participants engage in a seemingly unrelated exercise that primes them toward a particular goal. In a study by Rasinski and colleagues, respondents completed a vocabulary task first, matching either neutral words (e.g., blend, common) or words related to the goal of being honest (e.g., genuine, honest, sincere, truthful) with a key word they were given.[13] They were told that their task was to read each word they were given and then indicate which of the following three words

---

[11] See, e.g., Tsuchiya (2005); Ahart and Sackett (2004); Corstange (2009).
[12] Tsuchiya, Hirai, and Ono (2007).
[13] Rasinski et al. (2005).

was most similar to the first. The words were all similar in meaning so careful scrutiny was necessary to differentiate them. As predicted, the authors found that those primed to think about honesty *before* self-reporting sensitive behaviors admitted to engaging in far more of these activities than the control condition.

Another effort to improve the accuracy of self-reports was directed toward resolving the well-known puzzle regarding how many heterosexual sex partners men report relative to women. On national surveys, men report 2 to 4 times the mean number of partners that women do. These statistics cannot be accurate for obvious reasons; each new sexual partner for a man is also a new sexual partner for the woman. Most researchers suggest that it reflects either intentional over-reporting by men and/or intentional underreporting by women.

But another possibility is that men and women use different strategies to generate their estimates, and these different strategies each bring their own biases. One survey suggested that men tended to use a retrieval strategy based on rough approximations or rate-based strategies (e.g., about 3 people a year for 10 years = 30 partners), whereas women tended to think back over time and count each partner.[14] Gender differences in retrieval strategies might account for the inexplicable gap to the extent that rough approximations lead to overestimation (because multiplying leads quickly to large numbers) and enumeration of individuals leads to underestimation (because people will almost inevitably forget some individuals).

Using a population-based experiment, Sinclair and Moore attempted to manipulate the kinds of retrieval strategies used by a national sample of adult, non-virgin heterosexual men and women.[15] They asked a third of the men and women in their sample, "Off the top of your head, please provide a rough estimate of your number of lifetime sexual partners." Another third was asked, "Please think back over your lifetime, starting with your first sexual partner, and count all of your sexual partners up to and including your most recent partner." A control group was asked the standard item known to produce a gender gap, "Please report your number of lifetime sexual partners."

Since I could not find any published report on the findings of this study, I turned to the TESS online archive and analyzed these data myself to avoid leaving my poor readers in suspense. I first removed a few extreme outliers from the data indicating number of heterosexual sex partners (those over the 99th percentile in the sample). A few were simply attempting to put Wilt Chamberlain to shame. Chamberlain famously claimed to have had at least 20,000 sexual partners, a total that was widely doubted, while one

[14] Brown and Sinclair (1999).
[15] Sinclair and Moore (2006).

survey respondent in this study claimed 99,999 partners, the maximum number one could fit in the open-ended response box. (Interestingly, this sexual braggart was a 44-year-old woman.) Having eliminated the respondents like this one, whose claims stretched all credibility, I used analysis of variance to compare the mean number of partners for men and women using the two directive strategies.

Consistent with the investigators' expectations, the "control condition"— that is, when people were simply asked to report a number of sex partners without reference to how to go about it—generated the highest number of partners for men (16.5) and the lowest number for women (6.8), thus producing the largest gap between the two groups (9.7). Asking both men and women to enumerate individually increased the number of partners reported by women (relative to their default strategy), and very slightly reduced the number reported by men, thus narrowing the gap to a difference of 7 partners.

As it turns out, the best strategy for erasing the gender gap in numbers of sex partners is to ask both men and women to produce "top of the head" estimates without thinking too much. When this was done, the difference between men and women was reduced to an only marginally significant difference of 3.8 partners, with men reporting over 12 partners on average and women almost 9 partners. Although no single technique systematically increased or decreased the average number reported by both men and women, a significant interaction between the estimation technique and gender further confirmed that either directive technique improved upon a non-directive approach that left the two genders to default to whatever estimation strategy they were so inclined. In the end, of course, we cannot be sure that these are the most accurate estimates of the true underlying numbers, nor that social desirability norms are not continuing to drive the numbers apart. Differing inferential strategies may not be the only contributing factor.

In my own subfield of media and politics, one of the biggest measurement headaches has been caused by numerous, largely unsuccessful efforts to get people to self-report their exposure to political news. Relative to Nielsen estimates, surveys severely over-report news exposure, by a factor of 3 on average, but by as much as 8 times among some demographics.[16] Although over-time trends suggest that there is some signal within all of that noise, and survey estimates and Nielsen ratings go up and down together, the extent of over-reporting leaves analyses based on news exposure highly questionable.

---

[16] It is worth noting that Nielsen estimates have themselves also been challenged (see Li, 2009).

So why do people overstate their exposure to television news? One widely believed possibility is that people are embarrassed to admit how little time they spend monitoring politics and public affairs, and thus they systematically inflate their estimates for purposes of giving a more socially desirable impression. A list experiment was used to test the social desirability hypothesis, but results were not supportive.[17]

Another possibility is that people just do not try hard enough and thus end up "satisficing" with an answer that is sub-optimal. An additional population-based experiment was used to explore this possibility using an experimental treatment that encouraged people to think more carefully about their answer than they otherwise might. In this case, the experimental treatment read as follows:

> The next question is very important. After I finish reading the question, I would like you to spend at least 15 seconds thinking about it. I will let you know when the 15 seconds are up. If you wish to take more time, just let me know. Okay?[18]

Both experimental and control groups were then asked, "In a typical week, how many days do you watch the news on television?" As with the list experiment, the anti-satisficing treatment made no difference in the mean number of days reported.[19]

Use of Anchoring Techniques

Anchoring techniques begin with the premise that if respondents are given anchors or reference points, such as information about the frequency of the behavior in the general population, they will be able to estimate more accurately. In the study of self-reported TV news exposure described above, three variations of anchoring were attempted using different introductory statements. One cautioned respondents against estimating based on out-of-date information and established a vague sense of the population norm: "Television news audiences have declined a lot lately. Few

---

[17] See Prior (2006, 2009).

[18] Prior (2009).

[19] To give this hypothesis yet another chance to work, a follow-up was added that alerted respondents to just how difficult it was to accurately assess one's news exposure. Only 13 percent of respondents opted to reconsider their responses as a result, and more than half of them increased their estimates as a result, thus further exacerbating the overestimation problem. Their answers may have been impossibly high and invalid, but at least they were reliably so.

Americans watch the national news on a typical weekday evening." A second group received very specific information about the population anchor: "Television news audiences have declined a lot lately. Less than one out of every ten Americans watches the national network news on a typical weekday evening." A third treatment purposely pushed toward inflated estimates: "With all that's going on in the world these days, many Americans watch the national network news on a typical weekday evening." In general, any information about population frequencies or references to others reduced over-reporting.[20] Moreover, results suggested that people often inferred their exposure to news from their levels of general political knowledge rather than from actual exposure.

In a closely related measurement experiment, questions about political interest were purposely placed in different contexts by altering question order. If respondents received political knowledge questions first, then they systematically estimated lower levels of political interest thereafter. The difficulty they had in answering knowledge questions caused them to lower their self-estimated interest levels. This same effect lessened when the knowledge questions did not *immediately* precede the interest questions, providing further evidence that the knowledge questions were anchoring self-inferred interest levels.[21]

Survey researchers have long bemoaned the fact that the very same question can be interpreted in different ways by different people. The classic example of this comes from the Woody Allen movie *Annie Hall*, where a split screen shows both Alvie Singer and Annie Hall, each separately talking to their therapists about how often they have sex with each other.[22] Alvie responds, "Hardly ever; maybe three times a week," whereas Annie replies, "Constantly. I'd say three times a week."

The use of concrete quantifiers can obviously solve their particular problem (well, certainly not *all* of their problems), but often the situation is more complex. Anchoring vignettes have been suggested as a means of improving the interpersonal comparability of self-reports.[23] The basic idea is to have respondents self-report on the key behavior or attitude of interest, and ask the same respondent to assess hypothetical people described in short vignettes. The variation in assessments of the vignettes (which remain constant) allows researchers to improve comparability by rescaling respondents' self-assessments relative to their vignette responses.

[20] See Prior (2009) for details.
[21] See Lasorsa (2006) for details.
[22] Schaeffer (1991).
[23] King et al. (2004); King and Wand (2007).

In a population-based experiment extending the usefulness of an-choring vignettes, Hopkins and King asked half of respondents for self-assessments before assessing the vignettes, and half after.[24] When self-assessments followed the vignettes, respondents were more likely to define the response scale in a common way; the vignettes essentially helped communicate the question's intended meaning. The researchers thus concluded that to reduce measurement error, it is best for research-ers to ask respondents to rate hypothetical people first, and then to rate themselves.

These and other studies suggest that anchoring vignettes hold the poten-tial to reduce measurement error. The anchoring vignette strategy is likely to be particularly beneficial in cross-national surveys, where researchers often fear they are comparing apples to oranges, even with literal transla-tions of a given question. Anchoring via internal norms may be problem-atic for cross-national research, but anchoring vignettes may be able to communicate shared meaning across national boundaries.

The Utility of Population-Based Experiments for Improving Measurement

Experiments of all kinds are inevitably useful for purposes of improving measurement, but what makes population-based experiments especially useful toward these ends is the availability of external data to corroborate estimates of whatever it is you would like to measure. In a laboratory, we can easily find out if one measurement technique generates higher or lower estimates than another, but we lack a basis for claiming that one technique is more accurate than another. Whether it is perceptions of crime rates, risks, or news consumption, there are true answers for specified geograph-ical units that can serve as useful baselines. It is not necessarily important that a sample be nationally representative, so much as that available ex-ternal measures are available for whatever population is being sampled. When researchers are able to compare the best real world estimates of a behavior, such as voter turnout, with the results from a population-based experiment exploring measurement options, we have the greatest possible leverage on improving measurement, one that laboratory experiments with convenience samples cannot hope to simulate.

[24] Hopkins and King (2010).

Direct and Indirect Treatments

THIS CHAPTER COVERS what are by the far the most widely used and most flexible forms of population-based experimental treatments, direct and indirect treatments. What I call "direct treatments" are those in which the manipulation or intervention is precisely what it appears to be to the participant. Perhaps it is a counter-argument to the respondent's current position on an issue. Or perhaps the respondent is being asked to judge a photograph of a person. With direct treatments, it is easy for the respondent to see that he/she is being exposed to new information, a new argument, or some other intervention. Subtlety is possible, but only to a point; the experimental treatment is pretty much what it appears to be, though the respondent is probably unaware that other respondents are experiencing a systematically different version of the survey.

With indirect treatments, the relevant characteristics of the treatment are seldom as obvious to the respondent, or even to a third party who is reading about the design of the experiment. Instead, the goal is to indirectly induce an altered mood, goal, priority, or thought process of some kind through a treatment with other ostensible purposes. Indirect interventions are necessarily more subtle. For example, if a researcher wanted to increase the salience of a person's ethnicity, he or she could ask a series of questions about ethnicity in one experimental condition, but not in another. Likewise, if one wanted to induce a positive mood in some subjects and a negative one in others, the investigator could have subjects recall two of their happiest life events in one condition, and two of their saddest in another. Participants responding to indirect treatments generally do as they are asked, but are unaware what, if anything, this activity has to do with subsequent questions and responses.

Although the difference between direct and indirect treatments is a matter of degree rather than crossing a line, I use this distinction below to illustrate some of the creative ways in which treatments have been accomplished. Although these specific experiments could have been done as laboratory studies, my point in discussing them is to illustrate that treatments of these kinds can be executed remotely, thus making population-based experiments, and their advantages, possible.

Chapter Three

DIRECT TREATMENTS

Direct treatments have been useful in addressing basic research questions as well as applied, policy-relevant concerns. Some of the most innovative ideas that came through TESS made use of the visual and interactive capabilities of the Internet survey platform. For example, Oliver and Lee designed a study to examine whether judgments about obesity for minorities and women were the same as judgments for whites and men.[1] Respondents were shown a series of computer-altered images of people at different body sizes and asked to evaluate at what point the person was "overweight" and at what point they were "obese." The computer-generated bodies were either male or female and either black or white. These two between-subjects factors were randomly assigned to equal numbers of black and white males and females, so that each group of respondents was representative of their race and sex. Respondents hit a button on their keyboard and watched the image gain weight before their very eyes, and then stopped when they identified the point at which they thought he/she became overweight or obese.

It will not surprise most women to learn that people considered the female image overweight and obese at significantly smaller body sizes than they did the male image. The race of the image that gained weight had no effect, but the race of the perceiver did matter. Overall, white men judged bodies as obese and overweight at smaller body sizes than black men did.[2]

Yet another study employed visuals and interactivity toward an entirely different end. In politics, when one argues that voters "identify" with a given candidate, one generally means that there is some dimension of recognized similarity between the candidate and the constituent. Maybe he holds similar values, she comes from the same area of the country, or he worked his way up in a company in a similar fashion. But people seldom, if ever, mean by this that the candidate is well liked because of a direct resemblance to the constituent! Nonetheless, given the importance of perceived similarity to liking, Bailenson and Iyengar hypothesized that people might be more likely to support candidates who looked to some degree like themselves.[3]

Long in advance of the actual study, the investigators created a pretext for obtaining digital photos of potential respondents online. Their experiment then manipulated two factors in a 2 by 2 design: the familiarity of the candidate that respondents were asked to assess (well-known or un-

[1] Oliver and Lee (2005).
[2] See Oliver (2005).
[3] Bailenson et al. (2008).

known), and whether the candidate's face was morphed with that of the respondent or with that of another participant. The latter morphed photo served as their control rather than simply an undoctored version of the candidate, primarily because morphing automatically increases the attractiveness of photos by enhancing symmetry, eliminating blemishes, and so forth. Some versions of the experiment also involved additional information about the candidates, such as their political party or policy similarity to the respondent.

Results were consistent with the hypothesis to a degree; in general, facial similarity through morphing produced more positive feelings toward the candidates, but only when the candidates were unfamiliar, or in the case of familiar candidates, when the respondents were weak partisans or independents. Basically, when people lacked information or another basis for judgment, they used facial similarity as a heuristic to decide what they thought of a given candidate. When other information was available, facial similarity was unimportant.

Although one can see potential policy relevance in the study of facial similarity—particularly for candidates who are running for less high-profile offices and who are different from most of their constituents—other studies have more directly addressed policy questions. In particular, population-based experiments can provide a valuable tool for understanding how policy changes will affect public decision-making processes. For example, the structure of health plans may have significant effects on public health when it alters the decisions that people make about getting preventative treatments such as vaccines for themselves or for their children. Davis and Fant wanted to know whether people with employer-sponsored health plans would be willing to pay higher monthly premiums for their health care in return for having coverage for vaccines recommended by the Advisory Committee on Immunization Practices of the Centers for Disease Control and Prevention.[4] Currently, 15 percent of insured children and more than 30 percent of adults are underinsured for recommended vaccines. The investigators' underlying premise was that many insured people who do not have coverage for certain services will not be willing to pay for them out of pocket even though they might be willing to do so if it were offered in the context of a slightly more expensive health plan.

Their experiment asked respondents which health plan they would choose if their employer offered these options as a benefit of employment: an individual plan with a premium of $45 per month, a family plan with a premium of $179 per month (based on national data about mean employee share of monthly premiums), or no coverage at all. The sample was

---

[4] Davis and Fant (2005).

designed so that half of respondents were from a home without a minor child and half from homes with a minor present.

Those respondents who opted for some form of coverage in response to the initial question were then asked for their preferences among health plans that varied only in their cost and in the comprehensiveness of their coverage of vaccines for an additional $3 per month (for the individual plan) or an additional $6 per month (for the family plan). The more comprehensive plan would cover any newly recommended vaccine regardless of how many were recommended for adults and, in the case of those who initially chose a family plan, recommended childhood vaccines as well.[5]

Surprisingly, their results showed "a broad willingness (more than 75 percent of respondents) to pay the higher premiums" in order to obtain coverage of new vaccines as they become recommended for adults and children. Not surprisingly, this willingness was strongly associated with respondents' perceptions of the safety and effectiveness of vaccines. But knowing that they would be willing to pay marginally higher costs even though they would not pay for the costs out of pocket is extremely useful for those designing health care plans to maximize public health benefits.

Population-based experiments have been useful in understanding preferences on foreign as well as domestic policy. In the last fifteen years or so, the use of force by modern nation-states has come to involve not only the usual military organizations made up largely of citizens, but also private companies that provide military and security services that were once covered entirely by our country's military organizations. This alternative to a state-organized military became especially apparent during the Iraq war. Investigators Avant and Sigelman wanted to know whether having "hired guns" (that is, private security firms) fight in place of U.S. troops changes the way the public responds to deaths during a military operation.[6]

The researchers hypothesized that the deaths of private soldiers, commonly known as "contract soldiers," would elicit less of a response and less of a decline in support for the mission than would be the case with the

---

[5] After choosing a health plan, respondents were block randomized into receiving either a private gain argument or the private + public gain argument. The private gain argument advised respondents that new vaccines might cost $75 or more for each set of doses if paid for out of pocket, and that vaccines could reduce the need for physician visits and antibiotics. They were also informed that vaccines could cause some side effects and might or might not be recommended for the respondent and his/her children in particular. Those who received the private plus public arguments heard the same information as described above, but also were told that the vaccines might protect people who do not receive the vaccines themselves, so that even if the vaccines were not recommended for the respondents and his/her family, they were likely to benefit other members of their communities. Finally, they were again asked to indicate their choice of health plan.

[6] Avant and Sigelman (2006, 2008).

deaths of regular military soldiers. To examine this hypothesis, they presented two randomly assigned groups of respondents with identical stories about the deaths of Americans in Iraq, with the exception that one story said the dead were soldiers and the other said they were private contractors. A third group read a story about the rise of the security industry, and a fourth served as a control group. Subsequently, respondents were asked about their emotional states, their levels of support for the war in Iraq, and their perceptions of the motivations of public and private soldiers.

In the public soldiers dying condition, only 8 percent said the soldiers were motivated by material gain; most thought their motivations were either doing their job or serving their country. The control group was very similar in its distribution of responses. But among those who read about the contract soldiers dying, 27 percent ascribed their motives to material gain. In other words, military soldiers were motivated by patriotism, whereas contract soldiers were motivated by money for doing the same job.

Surprisingly, there were no differences in support for U.S. involvement in Iraq, nor differences in perceptions of how well things were going in Iraq, based on whether it was military soldiers or contract soldiers dying. Given the difference in perceived motivations, one might assume that using contract soldiers rather than military soldiers would lower the political costs of the war. To the modest extent that the soldier and contractor groups differed at all, those in the military soldier condition were more likely to say that going to war was a good thing, that it was worth it, and that the war was going well. As the authors summarized, "rather than exacting political costs, news of soldiers' deaths may, if anything, produce small political benefits that stories about contractors do not." The death of U.S. military soldiers communicates a symbolic message about patriotism and sacrifice that private contractor deaths do not. Policymakers hoping that "farming out" casualties would preserve public support for war may well be disappointed. The use of private contractors does not appear to decrease the political costs of casualties.

Another direct treatment oriented toward understanding the public's foreign policy attitudes focused on reactions to unilateral versus multilateral foreign policy decisions. Not surprisingly, Americans prefer to have the company of other nations when it comes to foreign policy decisions. Over two-thirds of Americans believe that "the United States should do its fair share," but only a minority agree that "the United States should continue to be the preeminent world leader."[7] In their population-based experiment, Todorov and Mandisodza hypothesized that Americans were largely ignorant of one another's views on foreign policy, widely believing

---

[7] Todorov and Madisodza (2004, p. 239).

that the public supports taking unilateral foreign policy action, when in reality it does not.[8]

Their experiment utilized three conditions to analyze the implications of these misperceptions. In the control condition, respondents simply reported their attitudes toward the role of the U.S. in the world. In the estimation condition, they also were asked to estimate the proportion of Americans endorsing either unilateral or multilateral action. In the information condition, respondents were told the actual proportion of Americans endorsing multilateral versus unilateral views.

The results largely confirmed the authors' hypotheses. Support for unilateral foreign policy action was indeed overestimated: "For example, while only 23 percent of respondents agreed that the more important lesson of September 11 is that the United States should work alone to fight terrorism rather than work with other countries, respondents estimated that almost 50 percent of Americans endorsed this view."[9] Moreover, misperceptions were associated with support for specific policies; respondents who perceived the unilateral view to be the majority were almost twice as likely to support invading Iraq without the approval of the United Nations Security Council. The authors concluded that widespread misperceptions of public opinion can drive foreign policy attitudes; in an area of low public knowledge, people tend to look to mass opinion for guidance on the best course of action.

In addition to policy-relevant research, population-based experiments have played an important role in testing several hypotheses from evolutionary psychology. To the extent that evolutionary processes account for patterns of observations, they should obviously be visible among the general population as well as college student samples. The generalizability of results (or lack thereof) across samples is thus particularly important to this area of research.

One evolutionary hypothesis that has received a lot of play in the magazines I read while at the dentist's office is the idea that men are more bothered by sexual than emotional infidelity, whereas the reverse is true of women, who care more about emotional fidelity. The original test of this idea, by Buss and his colleagues,[10] has been widely replicated.[11] The idea is that the uncertainty over the paternity of any given child, combined with the certainty of maternity, means that men and women will respond differently to the same relationship threats. In this line of thinking, men should become more jealous of their mates' sexual infidelity than the mates' emo-

[8] Todorov and Mandisodza (2004).
[9] Todorov and Mandisodza (2004, p. 323).
[10] See Buss et al. (1992).
[11] For example, Buunk et al. (1996); Buss, et al. (1999).

tional infidelity. Because women are certain of maternity, the greater threat that they face is that their mates will withdraw resources from their offspring. Therefore, this theory suggests, women are more likely to become upset by signs of resource withdrawal and emotional infidelity by their mates than by signs of sexual infidelity.

As it turns out, the studies providing support for this theory were based almost exclusively on samples of college students, thus restricting both the age and the extent of relationship experience of the respondents. Despite what they may think, undergraduates are not exactly the most experienced people when it comes to relationships. Given that most are under the age of 22, there is only so much long-term relationship experience that is possible to have by that age.

In order to pursue the ability to generalize these findings across a more representative sample of subjects as well as different outcome measures,[12] Sabini and Green designed a population-based experiment crossing type of infidelity (actual infidelity versus hypothetical infidelity) with two types of outcome measures.

Obviously the ideal experiment is not possible in this case. It would be unethical to hire your most attractive graduate students to cause infidelity among a randomly selected group of respondents (that is, unethical to both your respondents and your grad students!). So instead, the investigators asked participants who were assigned to the actual infidelity condition if they had been cheated on, and if so, if it was sexual infidelity, emotional infidelity or both. People could not be randomly assigned to experience different kinds of infidelity, but in this study they were at least a random sample of those who had experienced infidelity. As part of the design of this population-based experiment, this condition was randomly assigned at a proportionally higher rate, knowing that many people would be screened out of the study if they had never been cheated on. In the hypothetical infidelity condition, participants were just asked to *imagine* that a relationship partner has become interested in someone else, as in the original studies.

Overall, results suggested that men and women are more similar than different. Both men and women showed more anger and blame over sexual infidelity than emotional infidelity, but both men and women reported more hurt feelings over emotional infidelity. As both a female and a follower of contemporary American politics, I could not help but think about these findings when pondering why then-New York Governor Elliot

---

[12] Critics of this theory have argued that more specific emotional components of jealousy should be tapped rather than "distressed" or "upset," terms which might mean different things to different people (Green and Sabini 2006; see also Sabini and Silver 2005). See Chapter 8 for details on how the dependent measures were also varied.

Spitzer's wife stood by his side at the press conference where he admitted infidelity, while South Carolina Governor Mark Sanford's wife evidently had something better to do that day. Most likely, it had to do with the greater hurt Sanford's wife experienced from her husband's confession to falling in love with another woman, relative to Spitzer's wife, whose husband admitted to sexual, but not emotional, infidelity. Given that sex and politics seem unlikely to become disentangled anytime soon, it would be interesting to know whether the *public* is also more forgiving of some kinds of transgressions than others.

In a population-based study intersecting both public policy and evolutionary psychology, Robinson and Kurzban tested the hypothesis that lay people have shared intuitions regarding the extent of punishment that fits a crime. On the one hand, they point out that "the common wisdom among criminal legal theorists and policy makers is that the notion of desert is vague and the subject of wide disagreement." On the other hand, there is some empirical evidence, mainly based on convenience samples, that people's intuitions of justice "are commonly specific, nuanced, and widely shared," cutting across both demographics and cultures.[13]

To assess the extent to which people agree on how much punishment is appropriate for which crimes, studies have had people rank order a number of descriptions of specific crimes based on whether each deserves more or less punishment than another crime. Is there truly a consensus in society on what is most (or least) blameworthy when it comes to the assortment of wrongdoings one might commit? Do people take the same extenuating circumstances into account in making these judgments?

Using a within-subject experimental design, the investigators asked respondents to rank a total of 36 different offenses in order of least to most serious. The first 24 offenses had to do with harm/theft and the remaining 12 were in other areas. Evolutionary perspectives hypothesize that certain content domains will elicit greater consensus because of a "universal, evolved cognitive architecture" for these domains.

A representative sample was used to test the generalizability of previous findings. In the theft/harm condition, the scenarios ranged from accidentally taking someone's identical umbrella, to an angry fan who head-butts and injures a fan of the opposing team, to one who steals whole pies from an all-you-can-eat buffet, to attempted robbery at a gas station, to forcible rape, torture, and strangling. Based on vignette descriptions, respondents sorted the offenses into degrees of severity by clicking and dragging each scenario on a computer screen to its appropriate place in the hierarchy.

The scenarios were purposely constructed to raise a variety of complex issues simultaneously, but the question was whether respondents would

[13] Robinson and Kurzban (2006).

44

still maintain a high degree of consensus along a unidimensional scale. As the researchers noted, "The scenarios included such offenses as theft by taking, theft by fraud, property destruction, assault, burglary, robbery, kidnapping, rape, negligent homicide, manslaughter, murder, and torture, in a variety of situations including self-defense, provocation, duress, mistake and mental illness."[14] Just a few examples illustrate the level of nuance respondents were asked to take into account when considering the culpability of the person who committed the crime:

Another person slips a drug into John's food, which causes him to hallucinate that he is being attacked by a wolf. When John strikes out in defense, he does not realize that he is in fact striking a person, a fact confirmed by all of the psychiatrists appointed by the state, who confirm that John had no ability to prevent the hallucination.

While a family is away for the day, John breaks in through a bedroom window and rummages through the house looking for valuables. He can only find an 18-inch television, which angers him. When he gets it outside, he realizes that it is an older model than he wants, so he smashes it onto the driveway, breaking it into pieces.

John is offended by a woman's mocking remark and decides to hurt her badly. At work the next day, when no one else is around, he picks up a letter opener from his desk and stabs her. She later dies from the wound.

A local farmer wakes up in the middle of the night to strange noises coming from the barn. As he gets up to investigate, he discovers John having vigorous intercourse with one of the farmer's sheep.

John is driving to see a man about buying an illegal gun but must baby-sit his friend's toddler son. It occurs to him that it is too hot to safely leave the toddler in the car, but he decides to leave him anyway and to return soon. He gets talking with the seller, however, and forgets about the toddler, who passes out and dies.

Aside from convincing respondents as well as the rest of us that John is one busy guy and an all around bad dude, what was learned from this study?[15] Surprisingly, the investigators found a high degree of consensus even with this far more diverse population sample. There was strong consensus on the rank ordering of the scenarios involving theft and harm, but

---

[14] Robinson and Kurzban (2007, p. 1867).
[15] Within TESS, this became affectionately known as the "Sheep Study."

considerably less consensus when it came to issues involving drugs and reproductive rights.

The benefits of population-based experiments and direct treatments in particular are not limited to policy-relevant domains nor to evolutionary psychology, but they are particularly evident whenever scholars want to make generalizations about how large, diverse groups such as "people" work. Even generalizations about smaller, but internally diverse groups, such as men, women, racial groups, and so forth, are often difficult to make without the benefit of representative samples.

Eaton and Visser took advantage of the diversity of national samples of men and women to study how the two genders might enact power roles differently.[16] In order to remain consistent with their roles, people in high power roles are supposed to be difficult to persuade; the norm is for those with high power to stick to their guns and resist persuasion. Those in positions of less power should be more likely to reconsider; low power positions carry implications of malleability and openness to influence. But do men and women enact high power roles in the same way?

In their population-based experiment, Eaton and Visser guessed probably not. They anticipated that men would conform to this general pattern, but that women in high power positions would continue to process persuasive arguments and even be influenced by strong persuasive arguments. They tested this idea in the context of a 2 by 2 by 2 experiment crossing gender of respondents (male/female) by power (primed/control) by persuasive message (strong/weak), using subjects who had already registered positive attitudes toward the death penalty during a previous interview. Respondents were exposed to weak or strong arguments against the death penalty (with strength determined by their experimental condition), and power was semantically primed by having respondents complete a vocabulary task that either did not involve any power-related words (the control condition) or that included words such as "authority" and "powerful." Respondents also registered their opinions on capital punishment after the arguments were presented, thus producing a repeated-measures factor for tapping attitude change.

In the control condition, both men and women were more persuaded by the strong argument than the weak one. But in the conditions where they were primed with the concept of power, the men did not demonstrate argument-quality differentiation. In contrast, the women in the high power condition changed attitudes based on the quality of the argument presented, becoming more persuaded by strong than weak arguments. "Powerful" men were simply stubborn regardless. The implications are that men and women think about and enact their power roles in different ways.

[16] Eaton and Visser (2008).

For men, but not for women, power means being resolute and impervious to persuasion. Interestingly, for women the effects of the power prime on persuasion were moderated by women's household income. High-income women resisted even the strong persuasive argument, just as men did.

INDIRECT TREATMENTS

The many experiments I have reviewed in the section above obviously share very little except a fairly straightforward method of experimental manipulation. A stimulus was presented, and people reported their response to it. However, in all cases, the combined ability to make causal inferences while simultaneously generalizing to a large, diverse population sample expanded the research knowledge in the investigators' respective fields. In some cases, however, people are not altogether aware of what it is they are being exposed to. For example, the power priming manipulation described above is not as direct a treatment as the persuasive arguments treatment. The issue is not so much deception as whether a treatment is being used for purposes of manipulating something other than its most obvious superficial purpose.

False feedback studies are a type of indirect treatment in which respondents are asked to engage in a task and are then provided with false (or by chance, sometimes true) feedback on their performance of that task. Given that such "opportunities" for self-evaluation are frequently offered via Internet these days (ever taken one of those online IQ tests where you supposedly get compared to Einstein? Yeah, right), this technique is not as odd or transparent to participants as it might first seem.

In one application of this technique, Knowles and Gardner manipulated respondents' sense of "subjective social connection;" it was suggested to participants that they were either social losers or social winners, supposedly based on the number of close friends they had just reported.[17] In actuality, they were winners or losers simply by virtue of random assignment. Respondents were asked about the number of close friends they had, and then were made to feel like they had fewer close friends than the average person or more close friends than average.

To accomplish this manipulation, simple pie charts were presented to each respondent. In the subjective social isolation condition, for example, respondents saw a pie chart showing that only 5% of people (labeled the "socially isolated") had five or fewer close friends. The pie chart suggested that those who had between 6-10 close friends were "weakly connected."

[17] Knowles and Gardner (2006).

Those in the subjective social integration condition saw a pie chart indicating that people on average had only two close friends and that only the most socially embedded people had three or more close friends.

The outcome of interest was the extent to which subjects subsequently tried to regain a sense of social connection by compensating for the experimental treatment. The researchers hypothesized that people who are (made to feel) socially isolated will fulfill their need to belong by inflating past group attachments, by judging their own social groups to be unusually cohesive and meaningful, and by forming non-traditional attachments such as those with television characters. After the manipulation, respondents answered a series of questions tapping attachment-enhancing tendencies.

Consistent with expectations, respondents used strategies such as group enhancement to regain a sense of social connection when told that they were social losers. But the actual number of close friends reported was a better predictor of whether people utilized these strategies than the experimental manipulation was, thus leading the authors to suspect that a stronger manipulation might be necessary.

In another study involving false feedback, researchers investigated the "ego-defensive hypothesis" that straight men will become more hostile toward gay men when their own masculinity has been threatened. Pryor and Ernst used a 2 by 2 experimental design to see if heterosexual men would express more anti-gay attitudes after their masculinity was threatened.[18] To accomplish this threat treatment, they designed a "Male Knowledge Test" including items that guys generally "should" be more likely to know. It included questions such as where the Heineken beer sold in the U.S. is made, the actual dimensions of a two by four, how often a certain filter on a car needs to be changed, the width of a football field, the kind of screwdriver that fits screws with hexagonal heads, and so forth—basically all the kinds of things that "real men" are *supposed* to know.

As the introduction explained it:

The following test was designed to assess your level of "Masculine Knowledge." Through the course of a man's upbringing and education, emphasis is placed on particular subjects. Learning these subjects is an important part of what it means to be masculine in our society. Women are encouraged to learn different subjects. As a result, by the time people reach an adult age, men are more knowledgeable of some subjects, whereas women are more knowledgeable of others. This test is designed to assess your level of knowledge of subjects that our society expects men to know. Some of this knowledge is practical

[18] Pryor and Ernst (2005).

or useful. Other parts of this knowledge simply reflect things to which men are typically exposed in our culture.

The test has been given to hundreds of men and women across the country. Through this extensive testing, we have developed a set of norms for men and women. After you have taken the test, you will see your score and how you did compared to other people who have taken this test. This test will measure your level of what we call "Male Knowledge."

In order to be certain that it is a threat to masculinity as opposed to a threat of any kind that produces their results, they randomly assigned men to receive either the Male Knowledge test or a General Knowledge Test, a series of items without any obvious gender association (e.g., about geography, what parts of a theater stage are called, the location of certain Native American tribes). In this case they were told they were being quizzed about "general knowledge" and that they were being compared to other adults.

After taking the "test," there was a mandatory pause with the screen indicating "Please wait. Calculating your score," and then the men received "feedback" on their performance on the test. The bar graph displayed suggested either that they did significantly below average or just about average on the test just taken. Subsequently, they were asked items about seemingly unrelated topics such as attitudes toward members of the Islamic faith before a later assessment of attitudes toward homosexuals.[19]

Precisely because it is false, false feedback requires debriefing. In addition, whenever researchers purposely make people feel uncomfortable or misrepresent the truth, the issue of harm to human subjects must be raised. I discuss this topic more thoroughly in Chapter 6, but if these are forms of discomfort that also occur in the course of everyday life for this population, then they are probably not particularly harmful relative to the beneficial contributions to knowledge that the research produces. This particular test makes my husband, and probably most male academics, a bit anxious because they score objectively poorly on the Male Knowledge Test. *False* feedback probably would not even have been necessary for this group. Whether they run for the remote control in order to reassert their masculinity is another issue entirely.[20]

---

[19] Although I have not seen these results in print, one of the authors communicated via email that he thought they had null results, thus explaining the lack of publication thus far.

[20] Men's worldwide dominance of the remote control remains theoretically underexplored, although it has been alternatively linked to a desire to control situations, to an anatomical affinity, and to the male desire to maintain distance from their activities (see Center for Media Literacy, http://www.medialit.org/reading_room/article36.html).

Not all indirect treatments need to involve deception, however. In fact, most of them surreptitiously "prime" or bring to mind a particular consideration without any misrepresentation. Such is the case in an indirect treatment that was implemented among a sample of European Americans and African Americans. Psychiatrists have noted that African Americans score unusually high on common self-report screening scales tapping anxiety related to obsessive-compulsive disorder (OCD). OCD inventories ask for endorsement or rejection of statements such as, "I find it difficult to touch an object when I know it has been touched by strangers," and "I sometimes have to wash or clean myself simply because I think I may be dirty or 'contaminated.'"

Studies using college student samples have found that while these screening tools are highly predictive of actual distress and dysfunction due to contamination anxiety for European Americans, they have little predictive validity for African Americans. For example, follow-up interviews with black and white students suggest that most of the high-scoring African Americans do not actually meet the standards for OCD.

The question is, why? Why do African Americans report greater concern about washing and cleaning than Europeans Americans? One possibility is that African Americans and European Americans simply have different cultural norms, with African Americans placing greater emphasis on cleaning, grooming and so forth, thus producing a higher number of positive endorsements on the OCD inventories.[21] But another possibility is suggested by studies of "stereotype threat" in which the salience of group identity alters group members' behaviors.[22] For example, girls do worse on math tests if primed by statements like the infamous Teen Talk Barbie's admonition, "Math is hard!" Fortunately, Barbie has since been silenced. But similar findings demonstrate that reminding people of stereotype-linked identities can alter their behaviors. For example, Asians do better on math tests if they are reminded about the positive stereotype of their ethnic group.

To date, stereotype threat had been examined strictly in relation to academic or athletic performance. However, based on this same general idea, Williams and colleagues wondered whether African Americans were over-compensating for negative stereotypes by over-endorsing cleaning items to improve self-presentation; in other words, this discrepancy could result from an unconscious desire on the part of African Americans to self-present in a counter-stereotypical manner.[23] The authors dubbed this possibility "stereotype compensation" and noted that segregationist statutes

[21] Williams and Turkheimer (2007).
[22] Steele (1997).
[23] See Williams et al. (2008).

preventing blacks and whites from using the same facilities were explicitly based on the assumption that sharing facilities would contaminate European Americans. To the extent that African Americans unconsciously seek to counter such stereotypes, it may result in over-endorsement of OCD-indicative items.

Using a population-based experiment, Williams sought to determine whether the same pattern of differences observed among college students would also hold in a national sample. Toward this end, their sample was stratified to be half European American and half African American (Hispanics and those of mixed racial backgrounds were not included), and a randomly assigned experimental manipulation determined whether respondents were asked about their ethnic and racial identity and degree of ethnic identification *before* the OCD scales or *after*. By asking questions about race *before* asking questions about contamination anxiety, the investigators hoped to determine whether increasing the salience of racial identity exacerbates differences in the scales between African and European Americans.

The results were incontrovertible. African Americans scored higher on average on every single item as well as on the overall index. For whites, it made no difference if ethnicity was made salient or not; their means remained the same. But blacks whose ethnicity was made salient before the OCD questions scored significantly higher than blacks whose ethnicity was not primed. Interestingly, people of both races from southern states reported significantly higher levels of contamination anxiety. The authors concluded that the black-white difference in scale scores is a highly generalizable phenomenon. Unfortunately, this means the standardized scales are of little use for purposes of screening African Americans for OCD.

One final example further illustrates the use of indirect manipulation without deception. Perhaps not surprisingly, how happy we are about our marriages is not simply a function of "marrying well" as the old adage has it. It is also a function of, among other things, our own levels of self-esteem and the way that we integrate information on the good and the bad aspects of our relationship partners. People with high self-esteem tend to integrate information about their partners' faults and virtues so they are linked in memory, whereas those with low self-esteem do not—at least based on convenience samples.

Graham and Clark wanted to see if these same associations between high self-esteem, integrative thinking, and marital satisfaction held in a nationally representative sample of married people as opposed to a convenience sample, and it did.[24] Next, in order to test the causal proposition

---

[24] Graham and Clark (2006).

that non-integrated thinkers will have perspectives on their marriages that are more dependent upon the immediate context, the investigators randomly assigned married respondents to recall either three positive marital events or three negative ones. Their hypothesis was that the positive and negative manipulations should have a greater impact on levels of marital satisfaction for those who are non-integrated thinkers because of their limited tendency to integrate the good and the bad in their minds. By linking the original descriptive finding (high self-esteem goes along with marital satisfaction), these researchers were able to test a specific hypothesis to help explain that relationship.

EXTENDING THE IMPACT OF DIRECT AND INDIRECT TREATMENTS

Direct and indirect treatments are highly flexible and can be used to test hypotheses of all kinds. Researchers can implement not only random assignment, but also card sort techniques, false feedback, and just about any treatment that occurs in the lab. As I discuss in the next chapter, even confederates can be integrated into population-based experimental designs.

What is notable about population-based survey experiments that are policy-relevant is that they hold the potential to vastly increase the impact of social science research on public policy. Consider, for example, a social scientist who has completed a study with strong relevance to public policy. Let us say it is a well-executed experiment conducted in a university social science lab that makes a convincing case for its findings and the theory underlying them. Nonetheless, the researcher will be hard pressed to find a policymaker who is willing to implement a change based on "a bunch of college students in [insert university town here]," as the usual complaint goes. Even if it is not a well-founded concern, policymakers and those outside of academe find it easier to justify a change that has been tested on the same population that is affected by it. This gives population-based experiments an automatic leg up on other approaches when it comes to policy-relevant research that will ultimately be implemented.

As illustrated by the many examples in this chapter, most experimental treatments that can be executed in social science laboratories can also be administered remotely via telephone or Internet to randomly selected members of the relevant population. The significance of this ability should not be passed over lightly. In 1976, Cook and Campbell lamented that the most powerful, but least feasible way to increase external validity would be to execute experiments on random samples from the population to which a given theory was assumed to generalize. Given how impractical this seemed at the time, they suggested instead aiming for purposely hetero-geneous groups of people and settings so that "'quasi-representativeness' would replace more 'formal representativeness' of the random sampling model."[25] As the preceding studies demonstrate, this is no longer an im-practical pipe dream.

[25] Cook and Campbell (1976, p. 236).

Vignette Treatments

 Onne of the advantages of large-scale population-based experiments is the ability to do multi-factor experiments and test complex interactions. The relatively large sample sizes afforded by surveys mean that researchers can, if they so choose, have samples well into the thousands, thereby avoiding embarrassingly small cell sizes in studies with a large number of conditions. This advantage enables researchers to incorporate many experimental treatments simultaneously into a single experiment, and thus affords the opportunity to study complex interactions.

The vignette approach to treatment described in this chapter is especially well-suited to complex factorial experiments. Although this approach can certainly be used for very simple studies as well, the trade-offs that they impose—namely, the introduction of what are essentially hypothetical people and situations—may be most beneficial when studying more complex theories.

Vignettes could be considered a subspecies of direct treatment in that the interventions are essentially what they appear to be on the surface. But as a result of the simultaneous use of multiple independent experimental factors, all combined within a complex factorial design, there is less risk that the respondent's attention will be unduly focused on one factor, and thus the treatment may be less obtrusive from the perspective of the respondent.

The goal of vignette treatments is to evaluate what difference it makes when the actual object of study or judgment, or the context in which that object appears, is systematically changed in some way. For example, a victim of a crime might be described as male in one scenario and female in another, or black in one case and white in another, or wealthy in one scenario and poor in another, and the researcher may be interested in whether these factors cause respondents to be more likely to blame the victim for his or her predicament.

The object of judgment in a vignette treatment might be a policy, a person, or any object whose attributes are systematically varied across experimental conditions. Practically speaking, vignettes are made possible by random number generators embedded in software programs that can simultaneously vary multiple dimensions of the description that is offered to respondents. In telephone surveys, the interviewers simply read the computer-generated description that is randomly assigned to a given respondent from an interview screen using computer-assisted telephone interview programs. When respondents self-administer surveys via computers, the software likewise presents them with a single version of the vignette, so that they are unaware of the systematic variations that others may receive.

Technology now makes it possible to manipulate experimental factors within a vignette study using words, pictures, or a combination thereof. Using a standard randomization scheme, respondents are randomly assigned to receive a single vignette (assuming a between-subject design) or multiple ones (in a within-subject design). When vignettes describe other individuals, respondents are often subsequently asked to make third person judgments about the people described. In other cases, they are asked to imagine themselves in a hypothetical situation and then report how they would act. In still other scenarios, the respondent might be put in the role of policymaker or judge, deciding how much to reward or punish another person, for example.

Rather than describe this technique in the abstract, the best way to understand the potential of vignette treatments is by example. In a study extending the results of Sniderman and colleagues (described in Chapter 1),[1] Pager and Freese examined whether public attitudes about assistance for the unemployed were affected by the race of the person considered (white, black, or unspecified), the reason for their unemployment (laid off, fired, or incarcerated) and the prior work history (stable or unstable) of an unemployed 26-year-old male. As their vignette described him,

> Michael is a twenty-six year old [black / white / no race specified] male with a high school degree. About two years ago, Michael was [laid off from work / fired from his job / sent to prison for a felony conviction]. Prior to [getting laid off / being fired / going to prison], Michael [had held down a steady job for a few years / had trouble holding down a job for more than a few months]. Since he [lost his job / was released], Michael has been actively seeking employment, but has had great difficulty landing a job.[2]

This experiment included three independent factors: the race of the prospective recipient, the reason for unemployment, and work history prior to unemployment, combining to form a 3 by 3 by 2 factorial design,

[1] See Sniderman et al. (1991) and Sniderman and Piazza (1993).
[2] Pager and Freese (2004, p. 4).

with 18 conditions in total. Although previous vignette studies where race was varied have rarely included a race-unspecified condition, it proved useful as a neutral baseline for evaluating differences in reactions to white versus black versions of Michael. After hearing the vignette, respondents were asked: "The government often proposes job training and placement programs to help persons find work. How much government help, if any, should Michael be eligible to receive while looking for a job?—a lot, some, or none at all?"

Overall, respondents were almost 30 percent more likely to support the provision of "a lot" of government assistance when the respondent was black than when the respondent was white. Moreover, black recipients were favored over white recipients among both white and black respondents. Culpability also mattered a great deal, with fired or imprisoned workers less likely to be offered support than those who were laid off. Black and white respondents differed a great deal, however, in how previous imprisonment affected their willingness to help.

In interpreting these findings, Pager and Freese considered two possibilities. Either the survey respondents were giving what they assumed to be more politically correct and socially appropriate answers to these questions, or both blacks and whites believed that the historical disadvantages suffered by blacks make them more deserving of government help than whites.

Opinions differ about just how unobtrusive vignettes are. On the one hand, in this example, they clearly avoid respondents' awareness of comparisons on the basis of race. After all, each person is asked about one and only one prospective recipient, so there appears to be no potential for comparison. Indeed, it is impossible to identify any given *individual* in the study as racially discriminating given that comparisons can only be made in the aggregate. Even so, it is possible that respondents are aware that the race of the hypothetical individual has been explicitly mentioned and may therefore try to compensate when the potential recipient is black for fear of appearing racist. Because any given vignette can only mention a finite number of characteristics, focusing respondent attention on those characteristics alone may sensitize respondents in the way they respond. As discussed more thoroughly later in this chapter, combining text with photographic treatments can make this less problematic.

Although race-related judgment is an area in which vignettes are of obvious utility, they are far from the only research topic that has benefited from this approach. One area of law that remains largely unresolved is whether a person who is put at risk because of another person's bad behavior deserves compensation. When a person knowingly puts another person at risk, should the aggrieved person be compensated even if they are never actually injured? Typically, the law provides compensation for injury. But should a reduced probability of a healthy life in the future constitute injury?

As Darley and Solan describe it:

> This study asks subjects to react to a story in which fumes, which are released from a factory that manufactures glue, cause an increased risk of stroke in people taking a certain medication. An individual on that medication is exposed to the fumes. Half the subjects are told that the person exposed actually has a stroke. The other half are told only that the possibility of stroke has increased.[3]

The increase in risk is said to be more than 50% over a five-year period for half the subjects, while the other half is told it will increase to about 25%. The authors chose 50% risk as a threshold for awarding damages because it is a cut-off that some courts have already used.

Consistent with the typical use of vignette treatments, the extent of injury or risk of future injury is but one of several factors that are systematically altered. Given that previous studies suggest that people's judgments about such an incident will differ based on whether the person in charge of the manufacturing process knew what he or she was doing at the time, the vignettes also systematically varied whether the manufacturing manager was knowing (he knew the fumes would be released, but did not stop the process), negligent (he carelessly allowed the fumes to be released, but would have stopped the process had he been aware of its failure), or innocent (the release was not his fault). Thus, the vignette comprised a 2 (stroke/no-stroke) by 2 (likelihood of stroke) by 3 (perpetrator's state of mind) between-subject design, with subjects receiving one of twelve different versions of the incident.

Interestingly, the findings showed that in assigning penalties or awarding damages, people care a lot about the perpetrator's state of mind, and they penalized negligent and knowing perpetrators even when no harm to others actually occurred. In addition, even though some perpetrators were just lucky and by chance no injuries occurred, people still awarded lesser penalties and damage awards to potential victims in these cases. People also seemed to differentiate corrective and retributive justice, awarding compensatory damages based on the harm done, and punitive damages based on the perpetrator's intent and degree of negligence.[4]

In this study, the investigators were very straightforward in giving respondents many relevant pieces of information, and most of the information had an experimental purpose within the study, so they wanted all

---

[3] Darley and Solan (2005).
[4] Darley, Solan, Kugler and Sanders (2007).

respondents to process the information as carefully as possible. In other vignette studies, however, researchers must walk a fine line between making sure the relevant treatments are processed by respondents, and not calling undue attention that might trigger awareness of the study's underlying purpose. If the treatment is so deeply buried in the vignette that no one notices it, the manipulation check will not be significant; if it is emphasized too strongly, then respondents may become sensitized to the purpose of the study and respond in what they see as a socially appropriate fashion.

Studies addressing stigma of all kinds must grapple with this issue. One recent vignette study addressed whether relatives and family members of people with mental illnesses or substance abuse problems are harmed by the stigma associated with these afflictions. Little is actually known about the extent to which stigma associated with various kinds of problems extends to perceptions of family members (or to which family members in particular). Corrigan and Watson used a vignette treatment and systematically altered whether the family member was a parent, sibling, child, or spouse.[5] The affliction held by the family member was schizophrenia, drug dependence, or emphysema.

Their results suggested that the families of drug dependent people were most stigmatized. Further, parents and spouses were the most stigmatized family members. Contrary to expectations, the mental illness in the experiment (schizophrenia) turned out to be no more stigmatizing to family members than emphysema, despite the genetic tendencies associated with mental illnesses.

In another study of mental illness stigma, Wirth and Bodenhausen examined the role of gender stereotypes in mental illness stigma.[6] By varying the name of the person described in the vignette (Brian versus Karen), and the symptoms presented by the person (one of two gender stereotypic profiles, anorexia nervosa or depression for women, and ADHD or alcoholism for men), they were able to examine sympathetic versus intolerant reactions, helping behavior and so forth, based on whether the person with mental illness was experiencing a gender-stereotypic or gender-deviant symptom profile.

Overall, women demonstrated more helpfulness toward people with mental illness than men. But people's reactions were less positive when the individuals displayed gender-typical profiles of psychopathology. For example, when the person described in the vignette was male and had stereotypically masculine symptoms, or was female with stereotypically female symptoms, respondents demonstrated greater anger and less help-

[5] Corrigan, Watson, and Miller (2006); Corrigan and Watson (2007).
[6] Wirth and Bodenhausen (2009).

fulness. Overall, there was greater resentment and intolerance of stereo-typic offenders than non-stereotypic ones. This experiment provides an interesting result that begs for further interpretation via a follow-up study to explain these reactions.

Social scientists are often interested in identifying the boundaries of various social norms, as well as their consequences. But for obvious reasons, identifying social norms is particularly difficult using convenience samples, so population-based experiments are extremely valuable toward this end. One such vignette study examined how parents would react if their son or daughter became involved in an unplanned pregnancy.[7] Would the grandparents-to-be react differently based on the age or sex of the child who was involved in the unplanned pregnancy? Would they be more embarrassed if a daughter versus a son were in this situation? Less embarrassed if the son or daughter were older rather than younger? Mollborn hypothesized that to the extent that the strength of the "pregnancy norm" varies by gender or age, the family of the parent-to-be would be more or less likely to help with resources such as money, housing, and child care.[8] When a norm is violated, withholding help may be used as a form of behavior sanctioning.

The vignette in this case involved a hypothetical unmarried child of the respondent, described as either 16 or 26 years old, and either a daughter who becomes pregnant or a son whose partner becomes pregnant. Respondents were first asked about how they thought the child would feel, and then how they themselves would feel if the child were their son or daughter:

> [Jessica/Mike] is [26 years old/16 years old]. Last month Jessica and her boyfriend found out that she was pregnant. This came as a surprise to them . . . For the next questions, please imagine that [Jessica/Mike] is your own [daughter/son]. If you found out that [she was pregnant/his girlfriend was pregnant] and [she/he] was not going to marry [her boyfriend/his girlfriend], how embarrassed would you be when other people heard about the pregnancy?[9]

In addition to their likely level of embarrassment at this prospect, respondents were asked about their willingness to provide help, including housing, child care, and financial support.

Many survey researchers would suggest that asking people hypothetical questions such as these is a dangerous business because answers may

[7] Mollborn (2009).
[8] Mollborn (2005, 2009).
[9] Mollborn (2009, 127).

be highly unreliable; in addition, the experimental manipulations may lack the kind of realism necessary to produce valid reactions. Researchers can certainly ask questions such as "How would you feel if . . . ?" and "What would you do if . . . ?" but one cannot be certain the results are meaningful. For this reason, researchers are generally advised not to ask questions in purely hypothetical terms. In reality, there are people like the ones they describe, or else their study results would be of little interest.

In the study of pregnancy norms, the results indicated significantly greater embarrassment when the prospective parent was a teenager as opposed to a young adult, but no difference based on whether it was a son or a daughter. And consistent with the hypothesis about consequences, the more embarrassment about the pregnancy that was reported, the less respondents were willing to provide resources of all kinds. Unfortunately, the practical consequences of these reactions are that the very people most in need of help and parental resources are least likely to receive them.

It is, of course, difficult to know how one would react under these circumstances. My own teenager, while observing my husband happily carrying someone else's baby in a tummy pack, suggested to me, "You and Dad would probably be happy if one of us became pregnant!" Aside from convincing me that we have not done the best job of conveying social norms to our children, the response did make me think . . . how would I react? Most of us do not know, and even if we did, our initial reaction might not represent our eventual willingness to help.

But rather than throw the proverbial baby out with the bathwater and claim that this hypothesis cannot be examined experimentally, it is worth thinking about what might be done to increase the validity of people's self-reports about hypothetical behaviors. One possibility is to limit the sample in relevant ways, in this example to those with children perhaps, or even better, to those with teenage or young adult children. Even so, intent predicts behavior imperfectly, although they are usually significantly related to one another. But in this case the treatment had to be a hypothetical manipulation, rather than an actual one; I would not suggest that you even broach the idea of a real manipulation of this kind with your human subjects committee.

Another example of how population-based vignette experiments have been used to assess social norms occurs in a study of violence within families. Do Americans treat violence within the context of a married relationship differently from when it occurs among mere acquaintances? Does a non-violent social norm apply equally to women and men in our culture, as well as to married and unmarried people? To examine this question, Feld and Felson created a scenario in which the genders of the perpetrator of violence (the hitter) and of the victim of violence (the hittee) were systematically varied, along with the relationship between the two people:

Many people think it is important to stand up for yourself when someone mistreats you, but people have different opinions about what to do. I am going to describe a situation where someone is treated badly, and ask you whether you agree or disagree with several statements about what that person should do.[10]

The vignette goes on to say that John or Jenny gets very angry "for no good reason" at Beth or Ben, who is described as either a spouse or an acquaintance. John/Jenny swears at Beth/Ben in front of a group of their friends, and hits her/him hard enough to bruise her/his arm. In total, six of eight possible conditions were created by crossing the gender of the hitter by the gender of the victim, along with varying the status of the relationship from spouse to acquaintance. The two conditions involving same-sex married people were dropped.

Following the descriptions, respondents were asked about whether the person named as the "hittee" should hit back, how serious the offense was, whether the police should be called, and so forth. The investigators' hypothesis was that violence would be viewed more seriously when the perpetrator was male than female, and as especially serious when the perpetrator was male and the victim was female.

As predicted, under those circumstances respondents were more likely to say that the incident should be reported to police and that retaliation was appropriate. Interestingly, Americans were not more accepting of violence within marriage, and there were strong gendered norms against men hitting women. This pattern remained true even when the man was violently attacked by the woman first.

All of the vignettes described thus far have manipulated various factors using words. But some researchers have implemented vignette treatments using pictures instead of, or in addition to, words. Pictures may provide a less obtrusive, more subtle means of varying characteristics such as race or gender. Text-based vignettes in particular have been criticized for calling undue attention to certain characteristics and possibly triggering socially desirable responses. Pictures necessarily—seemingly unintentionally—convey certain kinds of information. Whereas race when mentioned in words seems intentional, race as conveyed by a picture seems unavoidable. This is an advantage for purposes of avoiding social desirability problems. It is impossible to show a face without conveying information about gender, race, and age, for example. Notably, the same lack of intentionality in communicating through pictures cannot be applied to some characteristics such as a person's dependability or mental health. But because of the

---

[10] Feld and Felson (2008, p. 696).

unobtrusive, self-apparent nature of pictorial treatments, their use is likely to increase as more population-based experiments are run via Internet.

Penny and Wilson used a combination of pictures and words in a multi-factor experiment designed to disentangle the direction of causality in the relationship between social organization within neighborhoods and the perceived quality of the neighborhood. For the most part, sociologists have emphasized the positive role of neighborhood organization in producing more desirable neighborhoods and communities. But it is also entirely plausible that people are more willing to get involved in their neighborhoods when they are perceived to be highly desirable; in other words, the reverse causal direction could be responsible for all or part of this relationship.[11]

In their study, they used pictures of actual neighborhoods as well as quotes from neighborhood residents to manipulate respondents' perceptions of the quality of the neighborhood. They then asked about respondents' likelihood of participating in certain activities if they were to reside there. By manipulating perceptions of neighborhood quality, the investigators were able to document the reverse causal path; that is, that perceptions of neighborhood quality can affect willingness to engage in community organizations as well as community organization levels affecting the quality of neighborhoods.

Pictures have tremendous potential as unobtrusive manipulations, but they are not without their own hazards when it comes to generalizability. For example, if one uses neighborhood photos as part of an experimental treatment, ideally they should be chosen from some larger pool of possible photos to ensure generalizability of results. The idiosyncratic choice of photos creates possible confounding influences and raises questions about external validity, problems that words may not pose.

One approach to addressing this problem was utilized in a study using Hurricane Katrina as a backdrop to study whether racial attitudes affect support for redistributive policies more generally. Fong and Luttmer told respondents that they each had $100 and that they were to make a decision about how much of it to keep for themselves and how much to donate to an organization that was helping Katrina victims, Habitat for Humanity.[12]

Respondents were shown an audiovisual presentation on the impact of Hurricane Katrina on a small town that was relatively unknown (either Slidell, LA, or Biloxi, MS). Using a series of slides accompanied by audio, the researchers manipulated perceptions of the racial composition of the town by showing photographs of mostly black victims or mostly white vic-

[11] Penny and Wilson (2006); Penny (2006).
[12] Fong and Luttmer (2009).

tims. A third (control) condition included the same photos but with the race of the victims obscured by filling in their images with blue coloring so they appeared as solid blue shapes, with the background left intact.

In order to prevent effects from using different photos of predominantly black versus white victims, the researchers matched the photos on age, gender, and the number of people shown. Further, they purposely reduced the resolution of the faces of the people in the photos so that their race is clear, but their attractiveness and other features are not. "Blueing" and "blurring" allowed control over the effects of characteristics of the different photos, which could not realistically be made identical on absolutely every characteristic save one. The audio portion of the presentation was used to manipulate perceptions of whether the city was economically disadvantaged (the city's income level relative to the national average) and the moral worthiness of the victims (by manipulating information suggesting they were or were not industrious folk).

Two main findings came out of their study. First, it mattered whether the victims were perceived to be living in an economically disadvantaged city. The less well-off the town was, the more of their $100 respondents were likely to donate. Counter to expectations, the average amount that was given to Habitat for Humanity was not affected by whether the race of the victims in the town was the same as the respondent's race. However, an item asking people, "How close do you feel to your ethnic or racial group?" was a strong predictor of racial bias in donations. Both whites and blacks who identified more with their own groups were more likely to bias their giving in favor of their ingroup.

Using a complex design involving both visual and audio manipulations, Fong and Luttmer disputed the argument that white people were less generous toward black victims. They nonetheless demonstrated that race does matter, just in ways that vary tremendously by individual. Although the photographs could not be identical on all characteristics except race, by carefully matching them on key characteristics and obscuring other details, they attempted to retain the same high level of control as word-based vignettes.

Strengths and Weaknesses of the Vignette Approach

What are the general advantages of the vignette approach? First, it is noteworthy that investigators utilizing vignettes are able to make causal statements about the impact of so many different experimental factors all in one study. For example, in the laid-off worker experiment described in Chapter 1, the authors manipulated race (2), gender (2), worker history (2), marital status (4), and age (3).[13] Importantly, the large scale of data collection offered by the survey experiment made it possible to execute an experiment with 96 different experimental conditions, a scale that is typically impossible in a laboratory.

Moreover, if this particular study had been done in a laboratory near my campus in Philadelphia, the ability to address the generalizability of findings as they did would have been lost, mainly due to a strong skew toward liberals in the surrounding population. Our recruitment strategy for laboratory subjects must go to great lengths to stratify by ideology in order to make sure we have enough conservatives as well as liberals, but this is often a losing battle, no matter what incentives we offer subjects. For a study with a large number of conditions, there simply would not be enough conservatives in the sample to draw conclusions about this group. Using a population-based experiment, this study found that the considerations for liberals were quite different from those for conservatives, and a laboratory-based experiment would easily miss this fact.

The vignette treatment also has the advantage of being a less obtrusive way of studying the impact of race and other sensitive issues on human judgment. Because race-based judgments and other stigma are considered socially undesirable ways of judging people, standard survey approaches directly asking people if such characteristics matter to them are unlikely to produce reliable results. With sensitive topics, the direct approach has very limited credibility.

With vignette treatments, on the other hand, respondents are unaware that the focus is on certain characteristics of the people or policy they are judging, and they have no way of knowing that other randomly assigned groups are getting subtly different versions of the same experience. They are simply responding to a given person, object, or policy, and others are responding to a somewhat different one. On the negative side, the respondent is aware of exactly what was (or was not) mentioned in the vignette, thus making the approach somewhat more obtrusive than one would ideally want.

Some of the key strengths of the vignette may also be tied to its shortcomings as an experimental treatment. Vignette studies are typically complex, full factorial designs; that is, they simultaneously manipulate more than one characteristic of the person, situation, or object about which respondents are subsequently asked for judgments. Precisely because there is a lot going on in any given vignette (that is, several experimental manipulations occur all within the context of one short description), it is unclear how much of the respondent's attention is focused on any one characteristic. This makes vignette treatments relatively unobtrusive, but

---

[13] Sniderman et al. (1991).

it also threatens their internal experimental realism—that is, the extent to which respondents are fully aware of and responsive to the characteristics in the treatments. The longer and more complex a treatment vignette is, the more one risks ineffective treatments.

Ideally, manipulation checks for each factor should be included at the end of the study after the dependent variables are assessed, thus providing evidence that the manipulations actually got through to respondents. But pretesting of the vignette is especially important for purposes of establishing in advance that the key differences are not so deeply buried in other details that they fail to be noticed. Ultimately, a balance must be struck between calling a high (and perhaps unnatural) level of attention to the manipulations, and burying them so deeply in other details that they will not be noticed at all by respondents. Because experimental findings will be useless and uninformative if the treatments fail, it is important to verify their effectiveness in advance and keep extraneous, distracting material to a minimum.

In addition to the potential dilution of a treatment's impact, another potential weakness arises when interpreting the effects of vignette treatments as indicative of policy attitudes. Vignettes often, though not invariably, feature specific individuals with a given set of characteristics. The investigator typically assumes that people's reactions to an individual will mirror their reaction to a collective bearing those same characteristics. If they support more government help for an unemployed person who is black than one who is white, for example, then it is natural to assume that they would also be more supportive of a policy that favors blacks over whites.

But judgments about individual people are not the same as judgments about collectives. A recent population-based vignette experiment provided some convincing evidence of this difference.[14] In a study of attitudes toward immigration policies, participants were shown a picture of a group of people having lunch at a restaurant, with pictures manipulating whether the skin color of the illegal immigrants was dark or light, and text describing the immigrants as either well assimilated into American ways of life or as maintaining a degree of cultural separatism. For the assimilated condition, the restaurant was said to be "Roy's Diner," as opposed to "an ethnic food market" in the unassimilated condition. Moreover, the people in the unassimilated condition were said to be eating "trays of spicy goat meat," but in the assimilated condition they ate "a platter of mozzarella sticks, onion rings and buffalo wings." Finally, assimilation was also manipulated by noting whether they were talking "in their native tongue" about "the new school they sent money to build back in their home country" or "the local [Montgomery, Illinois] baseball team's previous season."

[14] See Ostfeld and Mutz (2010).

Manipulation checks at the very end of the study indicated that both of these manipulations came through loud and clear. People who viewed the picture of darker-skinned people were more likely to say that the immigrants were probably from Africa or Latin America, whereas those who saw the lighter-skinned immigrants thought they were from Eastern Europe. Likewise, those in the high assimilation conditions considered the illegal immigrants significantly more assimilated to American ways of life than those in the low assimilation conditions.

So far, so good. But one additional, highly inconspicuous variation was also combined with this initial 2 by 2 design. A third, orthogonal experimental factor simply altered whether the group was described as "they" or "the Lina family." As the vignette continues,

> Yet beneath the apparent cheer of [their/the Lina family's] conversation is anxiety surrounding the aggressive lobbying by local advocates for stricter immigration laws. The most severe proposal would deport all immigrants who did not initially enter the country legally—regardless of reason—to return to their native countries and reapply for admission. For [this particular group/the Lina family], this would mean returning to the persecution of a military dictatorship.

> With the overwhelming sense of powerlessness that often accompanies being an immigrant, [they/the Linas] have resolved to continue working hard and enjoy any remaining time they have in the United States.

What difference does giving the immigrants a name, and thus personalizing them to this very limited degree, have on subsequent attitudes toward immigration policy? Given the hard line that many Americans take toward illegal immigrants, one might suspect that it would matter little, if at all, relative to the other treatments. The relatively sympathetic portrayal of these illegal immigrants (facing the prospect of a military dictatorship at home) should raise mean levels of pro-immigration support, but my co-author and I assumed that the minor level of personalization was unlikely to matter much.

We were very wrong. Race mattered not at all to the level of support or opposition to immigration that was elicited, except in combination with lack of assimilation. When whites viewed illegal immigrants who were both dark-skinned and unassimilated, it increased their opposition to immigration. But the personalized family versus anonymous group treatment made a consistent significant difference not only to attributions of responsibility for their predicament, but also to support for increased versus decreased immigration and a host of related policy attitudes. Respondents were consistently more sympathetic to the personalized group portrayal than to the anonymous one, despite the fact that the same number of people were depicted in both conditions, and despite the fact that the dependent variables asked about general policy attitudes, not about what should happen to this particular group of people.

Similar patterns of findings have emerged elsewhere, indicating a tendency toward greater empathy and support for personalized portrayals than for collectivist or anonymous ones.[15] The lesson to be drawn from these experiences for those interested in using vignettes is that it matters whether investigators design a study around asking about Mike, the schizophrenic, as opposed to a vignette about schizophrenics more generally. Individual experiences of adversity may elicit different reactions from people than abstract social problems do.

As social researchers, our interest tends to be in collectives rather than any specific individual, and yet the vignette approach often asks about an individual as a means of understanding policy attitudes involving larger groups. Whether personalization alters the means of the dependent variables without affecting relationships with other variables remains to be seen. But to the extent that personalization via vignettes *interacts* with the impact of the factors we care about, the results of vignette experiments could be misleading if the research interest is specifically in policies, which are seldom made with just one individual or circumstance in mind.

For many research purposes, however, the focus on individuals seems entirely appropriate because the behavior or attitude of interest is directed toward an individual rather than a group. For example, if one is concerned about the impact of stigma on individuals, then scenarios describing individuals and assessing what others think of them as individuals seems parallel to situations in which people might react based on stigma in the real world. Likewise, if one wants to know what effect an ethnic-sounding first name has on one's chances of getting a job interview, then it makes sense to have respondents evaluate and choose among individual résumés.

---

[15] Cao (2010); but cf. Iyengar (1987); Iyengar and Kinder (1987).

Treatments in the Context of Games

Y ET ANOTHER WAY that social scientists have administered experimental treatments is in the context of games, broadly construed. In some cases, these appear to be (or actually are) real games that people play for fun and entertainment. In other cases, these are economic games, which are typically played in a lab setting without an entertainment incentive so much as a fiscal one (thus making them a bit more like work). Such games may or may not have intrinsic entertainment value. In either case, I consider them "games" because the respondent engages in a set of interactions with other players, and the interactions are governed by certain rules that apply strictly to this specific context, which typically involves some sort of end goal or motivational narrative (e.g., getting the cheese, delivering the mail, slaying the dragon).

I begin with a description of how treatments have been implemented in the context of several classic economic games using random population samples. In these studies, the biggest challenge is adapting the often complex instructions and expectations to a sample that is considerably less well educated on average than college student subjects. In order to play and produce valid experimental results, participants in the game have to understand clearly how it works and buy into the realism of the experimental situation.

Accomplishing this is seldom easy when dealing with population samples that are highly diverse not only in terms of education, but also life experiences. For this reason, game treatments in population-based experiments are typically best implemented online. The telephone is simply too difficult a medium for purposes of explaining the rules of many games, and without visual imagery or written rules, it is difficult for respondents to fully comprehend and actively participate in highly abstract interactive decisions. All of the experimental treatments described in this chapter are implemented using computer-based interfaces that allow interaction, or at least the simulation of it. The presentation of written rules of the game on a screen is a definite advantage to this approach. But even more importantly, if respondents are part of an ongoing Internet panel, they know from their ongoing participation with the survey organization that they will be paid as promised, so the incentives are credible.

In the second section, I demonstrate that in addition to standard economic experiments, games also have been useful for their capacity to stimulate and simulate social interaction, either with a computer or with other individuals. These social games differ from economic games in that they are typically played without a purposeful goal of winning money. Because people who use computers are usually accustomed to the Internet as a means of communicating with others, social interactions using computers can be modeled relatively seamlessly, without arousing suspicion. After all, people play social games online all the time, so the context is not unfamiliar to Americans who use the Internet.

Finally, the third section of this chapter explores the potential—already well under way—for online "microworlds," also known as "virtual worlds" or "game worlds," to simulate real world experiences in a way that makes highly involving and complex treatments possible. Some would argue that the way people behave in microworlds is not the same as how they behave in the real world because it is "only a game," and thus implicitly question the generalizability of findings that might emerge from this research setting. On the other hand, as gamers will tell you, people now spend real money in microworlds, sell virtual goods for actual rather than virtual profits, and interact socially with virtual others. Generalizability remains an open question here as in many other experimental settings, and some types of outcome behaviors (e.g., purchasing) probably have more external validity than others (e.g., transmogrification). Still, microworld environments may allow social scientists to go beyond mere hypothetical consideration of system-level outcomes via computer modeling to incorporation of actual human behavior. To date, microworlds have not been used in studies that technically qualify as population-based experiments. Nonetheless, I include them in my discussion of game-based studies because it seems only a matter of time before microworlds are used to further expand the potential for experimentation.

ECONOMIC GAMES

Particularly in the realm of behavioral economics, a number of studies have tested hypotheses using population-based experiments for purposes of either generalizing results to more diverse populations, or to explore variations in how well a theory applies among subgroups in the population. Consider, for example, studies of trust. Trusting other people involves more than willingness to risk monetary loss; it also involves a willingness to risk feeling betrayed. People's willingness to trust another person (as opposed to trusting a parachute) involves the risk that they will be betrayed by that person, which is unpleasant and undesirable. When it comes to trusting other human beings, one must be willing to risk not getting what one expects, as well as the additional pain of knowing someone has purposely deceived.

In studies that used college students in a laboratory setting, Bohnet and Zeckhauser found evidence suggesting that ethnic minorities and majority white students were susceptible to different components of the experience driving their willingness to trust.[1] Willingness to take risks could be part of it, but so could the unpleasantness of being betrayed by another person whom one had decided to trust, or knowing that one had been treated inequitably by another. Based on findings from student samples, they hypothesized that members of minority groups were sensitive to different risks associated with trusting than majority group members.

Using a population-based experiment that stratified by minority status, the investigators designed a study in which a subject (Subject A) had to choose between a sure payoff and a risky payoff that could be either higher or lower than the sure payoff.[2] Participants were assigned to one of two conditions. In the Random Choice condition, if the risky payoff was chosen, Subject A was told the payoff was decided randomly by the computer. In the Person Choice condition, that payoff was decided by another study participant, Subject B, thus introducing the prospect that Subject A could be betrayed by Subject B, who would pocket whatever Subject A did not receive. Each subject played a series of three games, providing data on three separate decisions. The sequence of play meant that if Subject B was in the situation of having to choose which payoff to give Subject A, then it was because Subject A had already spared Subject B from the worst possible payoff.

Results suggested that betrayal in a trust situation is perceived as a worse experience than the equivalent economic loss due to bad luck; in other words, people were especially averse to economic risk if it was packaged along with betrayal. This observation is extremely important given that most economic transactions involve trusting another human, who also carries the potential for betrayal. When this effect was broken down by demographics, it appeared that certain subgroups, such as Caucasians, were more averse to betrayal than others.

For a subset of participants in the Person Choice condition, betrayal was replaced by inequality (Subject B makes the decision, but the payoffs go to Subject A and a third subject). In other words, the risk is not that B will betray A to achieve *personal* gain, but that B will be capriciously unfair to A. Results suggested that traditionally disadvantaged groups such as blacks and Latinos were most averse to the capricious inequality condition, while

---

[1] Bohnet and Zeckhauser (2004a).
[2] Bohnet and Zeckhauser (2004b).

traditionally powerful groups were more likely to fear betrayal at the hands of someone to whom they have handed over power.

An established Internet panel is especially advantageous for economic experiments of this kind because most have the ability to pay experimental subjects through an online account. Respondents are likely to have already experienced remuneration for their participation at various times in the past. In laboratory contexts, and particularly with telephone surveys, monetary incentives are limited in effectiveness unless respondents are truly convinced that they will receive payment consistent with the terms of the game.[3] Using survey respondents who have an ongoing relationship with a survey company alleviates this concern, although it raises others, such as panel conditioning effects. However, for the most part, these subjects are being used for straightforward survey data collection, thus limiting the likelihood of arousing suspicions about the purpose of an experimental study.

SOCIAL GAMES

The Internet offers a host of entertainment-oriented online games at many levels of complexity. Some involve interacting with computer-controlled entities, while others involve interacting with other people online who enjoy the same games. From very simple interactive games for youth to highly complex, strategy-oriented games, there are many opportunities to engage in interactions that demonstrate a range of socially relevant outcomes.

Unlike economic games, these games are typically played just for the fun of it, without the expectation of gaining anything of material value. Although I am old enough to remember the introduction of Frogger and Pong on the Commodore 64, I admittedly have not kept up with more recent games except in a limited way through my children. But in my capacity as an experimentalist, I have begun paying more attention because the potential for research via online games seems extensive. And now that I can no longer be promoted, I am free to spend time playing games with impunity on my office computer, with an eye toward the kinds of social science research questions they might be engineered to test.

This same kind of inspiration came to social psychologist Kipling Williams one day while he was being jilted during a three-way game of catch in the park. Williams found himself irrationally annoyed and hurt by the fact that after accidentally becoming incorporated into two other people's Frisbee game, thus producing a spirited three-way game of catch, he was

---

[3] This is the reason that pre-survey incentives are far more effective than the advance promise of payment for completion of a survey (e.g., Singer, Van Hoewyk and. Maher, 2000).

just as suddenly excluded from the triangle. The others abruptly decided to no longer include him in the game. Despite the fact that these were total strangers, he felt sad, angry, and embarrassed—in a word, ostracized.[4]

This paradigm—a three-way game of catch—became the basis for a game called Cyberball that Williams designed to study ostracism and social exclusion. He started with actual ball tossing in a lab, but the need to train so many confederate "catchers" made this setting cumbersome and inefficient on an ongoing basis. (Moreover, graduate students are typically not screened for this particular skill.) Instead, he produced Cyberball, a computer-based interactive ball tossing game that served as a minimalist paradigm for inducing feelings of rejection and social ostracism. The two other players in this three-way game were described as "other participants who are logged on at the same time," but were actually controlled entirely by the program.

One might be skeptical about the experimental realism of this paradigm. Participants were told that the game would help them exercise their mental visualization skills, which they would use in a subsequent experiment, as a means of assuring them that their performance in the game had no detrimental effects on their performance in the experiment itself. Animated icons represented the three players, and participants spent about five minutes playing the game. Once the respondent had a chance to catch and throw the ball a few times, he/she experienced (based on random assignment) either the "over-included" condition (having the ball thrown to the respondent on half of all throws, or more than their fair share), the "included" condition (one-third of the throws), the "under-included" condition (receiving only one-sixth of the throws), or the "fully ostracized" condition (receiving none of the throws).

Surprisingly, despite the fact that respondents knew they would never meet the two other people they were supposedly playing with, and despite the fact that their participation in the game had no consequences for them, respondents cared about the extent to which they were included. After playing, feelings such as mood, self-esteem, levels of belonging, meaningful existence, and control were assessed. Those who were included or over-included felt significantly better than those who were under-included. But those who were under-included still felt better than those who were in the fully ostracized condition, just as the authors expected. In addition, when people played Cyberball inside an MRI chamber, they showed greater distress and activation of the portion of the brain that registers physical pain when they were being ostracized.[5] Based on evidence of this kind, Williams

---

[4] An account of this incident can be found in Williams and Jarvis (2006).

[5] Eisenberger, Lieberman, and Williams (2003).

concluded that Cyberball "works" to create feelings of social ostracism; in other words, manipulation checks confirmed its effectiveness.

But is Cyberball a sufficiently powerful manipulation to use for studying the subsequent effects of ostracism on other behaviors? Apparently it is. The theory behind research on ostracism is that the pain and distress that people feel when being ignored, excluded, or rejected is adaptive for survival. Moreover, ostracism triggers individuals to "fortify their relational needs (belonging, self-esteem, shared understanding, and trust), which lead generally to prosocial thoughts and behaviors" that help them regain social acceptance.[6] Alternatively, ostracized individuals may reinforce their needs for efficacy and control by summarily rejecting others and increasing antisocial thoughts and behaviors. Both kinds of effects have been documented in response to the Cyberball treatment.

A series of additional studies tested the limits of Cyberball's ability to make people feel rejected. For example, one study demonstrated that even when told they were playing with a computer and not with other people, the game still worked to make people feel as if they had been ostracized.[7] Moreover, as demonstrated in the aptly titled article, "The KKK won't let me play," even when respondents thought they were playing against people they openly despised (i.e., the Ku Klux Klan), they still felt ostracized when the ball was not thrown to them.[8] Another variation of this game, called Cyberbomb, featured bomb tossing rather than ball tossing. Even then, being excluded from the game made people feel that they had been socially ostracized.[9]

The potential variations on this game are limitless, particularly given that the software is publicly available and can be programmed for alternative purposes.[10] A simple behavior such as throwing a ball in a game can be used as either a manipulated independent variable (by controlling how often the participant is included) or as an outcome indicating the participant's desire to include others. Rather than graphically represented players, some versions use player pictures, which also opens up possibilities of using Cyberball for studying discrimination and a variety of other topics. Other games present still more possibilities. In the case of the Cyberball experiments, the game serves as a means of implementing a manipulation. But different games could be used to implement manipulations of other kinds, such as making people feel more (or less) capable than others, or making them feel socially supported (or isolated).

[6] Williams (2007, p. 425).
[7] Zadro, Williams, and Richardson (2004).
[8] Gonsalkorale and Williams (2007).
[9] Van Beest and Williams (2006).
[10] Williams and Jarvis (2006).

Experimental manipulations are only half of the potential for using games. If validated, actions taken within games might also serve as indicators of dependent variables. In my own research, I have often wondered whether the desire to play Whack-a-Pol (a version of Whac-a-Mole that allows players to hit politicians and/or political animals) varies along with anti-government sentiment.[11] And what about Whack-a-Prof? Does it correlate with course evaluations?

My general point is that once behaviors demonstrated within the context of games are validated as indicators of real world attitudes, behaviors or emotions, or as effective manipulations, then games that people play "just for fun" may become valuable experimental paradigms for purposes of whole research agendas. The degree of control afforded via online manipulations and measures will release researchers from the need to spend long hours training graduate students in the finer arts of playing catch, and it may well be easier to recruit subjects into such activities as well. Because they are already programmed to work well on the Internet, online games are "naturals" as experimental paradigms that facilitate manipulations and as possible outcome measures.

MICROWORLDS AS CONTEXTS FOR EXPERIMENTAL RESEARCH

The kinds of online games described above tend to be pretty simple and straightforward; the frog either makes it across the street despite all that traffic or he does not.[12] But more recently, a more complex setting also has become the subject of debates about internal and external validity: virtual worlds, or microworlds. Microworlds are computer-generated environments where people interact in an ongoing way with the program and with others who are playing the same game. Some of the currently popular virtual worlds include Second Life and World of Warcraft.

Computer-simulated environments have existed for a long time for other purposes, mainly for simulating real world environments without the same degree of risk. Flight simulators, for example, allow users to interact with the program repeatedly over time in a way that is designed to be quite real. Likewise, recreational games such as fantasy or adventure games repro-

---

[11] As the Whack-a-Pol website puts it, "Stop the greedy political animals before they take over the White House! Whack-A-Pol is a fun game that gives you the opportunity to whack your favorite political animals as they pop their heads up all around the White House. Try to earn AIG bonuses wherever possible in this fast paced game." See http://www.gamespot.com/iphone/action/whackapol/index.html.

[12] For those who are too young to have enjoyed Frogger, the object of the game is to direct frogs to their homes one by one. To do this, each frog must avoid becoming roadkill while crossing a busy road, and then a river full of additional hazards.

duce an environment of some kind and allow the user to make decisions about their behavior that will lead to specific consequences, at least within the context of the game.

Advocates of the use of microworlds for social science experimentation point out that the complex dynamics that are possible in these worlds allow an unprecedented degree of experimental realism. In this type of study, computers are involved far more than as mere means of administering questionnaires, or of randomly assigning people to experimental treatments. More importantly, they make it possible for the experience to be complex and highly interactive, such that the environment itself changes in response to the participant's behaviors. Because microworlds can simulate dynamic processes over time, they have been argued to create levels of experimental realism that are seldom found in laboratory studies.[13]

For example, some epidemiologists have begun to think that online games might help them understand how diseases spread and, more importantly, how they might be controlled. The idea in this case came from something that occurred accidentally in the game World of Warcraft. The game creators introduced a new virtual creature named Hakkar, with the ability to cast a disease called "corrupted blood" onto others. The disease affected not only the person to whom it was directed, but could also spread to others in close proximity through virtual networks. Interestingly, the game creators thought that the severity of the disease and the limited period of infection would cause the disease to be self-limiting and die out. People would either recover or die, and the disease would quickly peter out.

Instead they got a naturally occurring pandemic plague that was out of control. As Strohmeyer described:

> Game administrators were baffled. As they scrambled to quarantine areas of the game world, the disease quickly spread beyond their control. Partially to blame was the game's "hearthstone" feature, which allows players to essentially teleport from one area to another, and which made it possible for the plague to reach the most distant regions of the map in just minutes.[14]

Just as the similarities between this outbreak and real world ones were fascinating, the dissimilarities also carried important cautionary tales. Who knew there was a downside to teleporting? And unlike many real world diseases, this one did not produce residual immunity if a person was lucky enough to recover. So characters in the game could become infected time

---

[13] Omodei and Wearing (1995).
[14] Strohmeyer (2005).

and time again, producing repeated cycles of infection and contagion. Moreover, it turned out to be a zoonotic disease; that is, it transferred to virtual pets as well as to virtual humans, and because it was not as lethal to pets, they continued to spread the disease all too easily. As with many real world diseases (think of swine flu), powerful characters were not seriously affected, whereas less powerful ones (think of children, the elderly, those without healthcare, and the immuno-compromised) were seriously affected.

This was not the first unplanned infectious virtual disease (apparently many Sims characters once died off from an infection carried by virtual guinea pigs that were inadequately cared for). But the parallels to recent world events made the research potential obvious. Asymptomatic ducks played an important role in spreading avian flu, just as air travel (rather than teleporting) made it difficult to contain the SARS epidemic.

Although questions relating to external validity give reason for doubt, virtual worlds are already being used as experimental settings for studying disease transmission. No one can reasonably argue that the way people behave in virtual worlds is the same as how they will act in the real world (any more than they can for laboratory research), but some types of behaviors and decision making are likely to be generalizable even if others are not. This potential is exciting to many epidemiologists (e.g., researchers could experiment with different perceived risk levels from diseases, different probabilities of transmission, and so forth to evaluate how these variables affect human behaviors). Given that the mixing patterns of some characters in these worlds are completely controlled by the programmers, there are many possibilities for testing what are otherwise abstract mathematical models of disease transmission.

Virtual worlds may not be "real" in the ideal sense that most social scientists would like, but the advantages of such an approach are many and obvious. For one, lots of people will not have to die. Many a human subjects committee could be persuaded that dying a virtual death, while extremely upsetting and disturbing, is still much better than dying for real.[15]

As mentioned above, microworld experiments have relied on convenience samples thus far. To date, two strategies have been used to execute experiments in virtual worlds. One is to build a virtual lab within the virtual world and recruit individual people off the virtual streets.[16] Non-thematic virtual worlds, such as Second Life, hold the best potential for representativeness given that people participate without regard to a particular shared

---

[15] Nonetheless, this distinction between real and virtual worlds is blurring as court cases erupt over virtual property and the value of online reputations (see Loftus, 2005; Dougherty, 2007).

[16] See Chesney, Chuah and Hoffmann (2009).

interest. Most concerns about generalizability center on the characteristics of online game players relative to the population as a whole, rather than the representativeness of the sample of players relative to the population of online players. Nonetheless, the virtual lab is an approach that could be executed by randomly sampling people at different times of the day and in different parts of the microworld.

The second approach to date has been to recruit subjects from another venue and induce them to spend a given number of hours playing an on-line game that has been reproduced in multiple versions with systematic experimental variations. Although this approach has been used only with convenience samples thus far (e.g., students), there is no reason it could not be used with a representative sample. Relative to other activities that experimenters try to induce experimental subjects to spend time on, game playing may be one of the most fun and thus also most likely to gain coop-eration from respondents.

In one ambitious undertaking, Castronova and colleagues created two equivalent microworlds called "Arden" in order to test the economic Law of Demand: does increasing the price of a good reduce the demand for that item if all else is equal?[17] Subjects were randomly assigned to play one of two different versions of Arden, and the only difference between the two worlds was that in one version a health potion said to "cure light wounds" sold for twice what it did in the other version of the world. Subjects spent roughly 10–15 hours in the microworld.

On one hand, manipulating the cost of a single item might be construed as a difficult target for such a test. Who cares about being healthy when it is all fantasy anyway? So what if my "light wound" festers into some-thing more serious? However, based on the results, the authors concluded that behavior in the microworld was "economically normal." Despite the fantasy game setting, and the fact that people were not playing with real money, people bought almost twice as many potions when the cost was low as when the cost was high. On this basis, Castronova and his col-leagues concluded that virtual worlds hold great promise for studying var-iations in economic systems. Still other evidence suggests that behavior in online environments obeys many of the same social norms as in the real world, thus suggesting that non-economic forms of social behavior in mi-croworlds also may be generalizable.[18]

My own sense is that virtual worlds are probably not ideal for many individual-level research hypotheses. For purposes of experimental con-trol, the rich, complex environment of a virtual world has many drawbacks. If, for example, one wanted to examine whether social pressure causes

[17] Castronova et al. (2008).
[18] Yee et al. (2007).

individuals to change opinions, microworlds would not be a good venue for such a test. Because subjects (masquerading behind avatars) are constantly interacting with other subjects in uncontrolled ways (along with some who are controlled by the game itself), a great deal of experimental control may be lost.

On the other hand, if the hypothesis under examination is at the level of a social or economic policy or political system, microworlds might well be the best way to go about testing it. Where else can an experimenter find a social system to manipulate? In addition, levels of experimental realism are undoubtedly quite high in online worlds, and people are easily drawn into high levels of involvement in their activities within them, as evidenced by the sheer number of users and the amount of time spent in virtual worlds. As of 2008, an estimated 73 million people were online gameworld participants.[19] Some specific online worlds have been known to attract populations that outnumber the citizens of Sweden.

Although these participants are not a representative sample of the population, they are becoming more so year by year. Moreover, with such a huge pool of users, samples could be constructed to be at least demographically representative via a stratified sampling technique. It is easy to bemoan the lack of representativeness of online game players, until one considers the paucity of opportunities and limited level of representativeness of field experiments that allow system-level manipulations.[20] Relative to many other environments in which experiments have been done, microworlds may be both more diverse and more representative.

Relative to traditional experimental approaches, the real strength of using complex microworlds for purposes of experimentation is in testing hypotheses about whole societies or systems within those societies. Virtual worlds have cultures that evolve over time, formal and informal social institutions, and economies that produce, consume, and trade in their own currencies, which can be exchanged for actual dollars. Entrepreneurs develop businesses (including a pervasive presence of people in the world's oldest profession), and a few people even produce personal income from their involvement in virtual worlds.

Although population-based experiments are not currently being executed in virtual worlds, they present opportunities for studying levels of analysis that experimental laboratories do not. The micro-level focus of experimental research has been a long-time target of criticism of this meth-

---

[19] Gaylord (2008).

[20] For example, Battalio, Kagel and Reynolds (1977) studied two experimental economies, a therapeutic token system in the female ward for chronic psychotics at the Central Islip State Hospital in New York, and the Cannabis economy established at the Addiction Research Foundation in Ontario.

odological approach, and microworlds may open the door to more expansive use of experimental methods. I suspect that policymakers in particular will find virtual worlds to be extremely valuable for understanding and predicting the effects of changes in public policy on human behavior. There is currently no better way to do experiments involving whole social systems on a longitudinal basis. Rather than cede this area to historians and observational research, scholars will want to take online games more seriously.

PART II

EXECUTION AND ANALYSIS

Execution of Population-Based Survey Experiments

POPULATION-BASED experiments do not fit neatly into pre-existing categories for research designs. For this reason, there is considerable confusion regarding best practices. This chapter addresses a series of practical matters involved in their implementation. The TESS staff learned a great deal from observing the execution of so many varied population-based experiments. Given the creativity and variation in designs, there are few "one size fits all" rules or admonitions for which one cannot find an exception. Nonetheless, there have been some useful lessons learned.

In this chapter, I hope to eliminate the need for others to learn the hard way. I use experiences from TESS and my own research to illustrate the kinds of problems most likely to plague users from different disciplines. Three practical questions are addressed in roughly the order that these concerns occur to researchers engaged in a population-based experiment:

1. How can I maximize the effectiveness of a treatment in a population-based experiment?
2. How should I think about measurement differently relative to designing a survey?
3. How do I explain this kind of study to my Institutional Review Board (IRB)?

At first glance these questions may not seem closely related, but I suggest that they are. The challenge of producing effective treatments involves simultaneously increasing the extent to which the independent variable is varied *and* reducing measurement error. If investigators can accomplish both of these things, they are virtually certain to learn something useful from the results of a population-based experiment, even if the underlying theory happens to be wrong. Consideration of ethics and human subjects comes into play because there are important limits on what investigators can do by way of manipulation in the context of surveys. Experimental design textbooks generally urge the use of strong treatments, the so-called "hit people over the head" approach. But human subjects committees are not going to allow investigators to hit people over the head—at least not literally, whether in the lab or outside of it. Producing a strong enough treatment can come into conflict with what the investigator and his or her IRB feel is ethical. Given that there are limits on experimental treatments, successful studies need to reduce the amount of noise in their measures as well.

Confusion surrounding these issues also arises because population-based experiments are neither fish nor fowl, so investigators tend to approach them from the usual perspective of either survey research or experimental research, depending upon what predominates in their own training. Not surprisingly, people from different disciplines tend to have different problems adapting to population-based experiments, and I will attempt to highlight the pitfalls that await new users of all kinds.

MAXIMIZING THE EFFECTIVENESS OF EXPERIMENTAL TREATMENTS

The major challenge in executing population-based experiments is creating effective experimental treatments. "Effectiveness," as the term is commonly used in discussing experimental treatments, can mean either that a treatment is effective in producing the intended variation in the independent variable, or it can refer to the effectiveness of the treatment in altering the *dependent* variable (i.e., the hypothesized effect). The latter type of effectiveness is determined solely by whether one's theory is correct or not, and there I can be of little help. My suggestions for effectiveness are specifically for purposes of increasing the effectiveness of experimental manipulations, that is, the variance in your independent variable, as typically measured by a manipulation check. Importantly, even when a theory does not work as hypothesized, the results are often still of interest so long as one can document that the treatment was, in fact, effective in manipulating the independent variable. Conversely, even when the experimental treatment *does* appear to alter the dependent variable, if the manipulation is not effective in altering the independent variable, this renders the findings indecipherable.

Manipulation checks are used to establish the effectiveness of the treatment, and textbooks on experimentation widely advocate doing so. Unfortunately, many a population-based experiment skips this important step, and thus undermines what can be learned from any given study. Whether it consists of a single item or a whole battery of questions, manipulation checks are essential to documenting that your population-based experiment accomplished what it set out to do. Experiments for which manipulation checks can be considered "optional" are relatively few and far between.[1] For example, suppose a treatment is a simple piece of information that is included in one condition but not another. Nonetheless, it is still important to verify that the treatment got through to respondents in the treatment condition and/or that it was not already known to a large extent in the control condition. This example is obviously a simplistic one, but it points to the importance of not *assuming* that a treatment has been received and processed simply because it is present in the flow of the survey interview. Particularly when administering treatments remotely, this is not a safe assumption to make.

Did we successfully induce lower levels of social trust, a good (bad) mood, or a more informed choice? Did the respondent read carefully enough to notice that the people described in the vignette were married or not married? Did the respondent see the children in the picture and notice that their skin was dark? Only a manipulation check can establish these answers for certain. In some cases, manipulation check items are inserted directly after a treatment, but more often they are included after measuring the dependent variable, so that the researcher does not call undue attention to the stimulus or create a demand for certain kinds of responses.

The importance of creating robust experimental treatments is even more crucial in population-based experiments than in the laboratory for one very basic reason: the sample of subjects is, by design, much more heterogeneous than in the usual laboratory experiment. If one reflects on what it takes to get a significant statistical result in an experiment, or even what it takes to substantiate a significant manipulation check, this problem should become abundantly clear.

The standard formula for determining whether one has significant experimental findings is the F-value in an analysis of variance. This value is equal to the sum of squared deviations from the grand mean *between* experimental groups over the sums of squared deviations from the mean *within* experimental groups:

$$F = \frac{\text{Sum of squares between cells}}{\text{Sum of squares within cells}}$$

In order to produce a large F-value, we need a large numerator that dwarfs the denominator in size. A small denominator is best obtained by using a highly homogeneous pool of subjects. But population-based experiments utilize precisely the opposite—a purposely heterogeneous group

---

[1] See O'Keefe (2003) for a discussion of situations in which manipulation checks may not be required.

of subjects. The dirty little secret about the appeal of college sophomores used in laboratory research is that they are attractive as subjects not only because they are readily available and cheap, but also because they are all the same along many dimensions. This homogeneity helps keep the size of the denominator nice and small. Thus a smaller effect size in the numerator is more likely to be statistically significant when the subjects are more homogeneous. Population-based experiments make it more difficult to document statistical significance in the manipulation check and in the experimental treatment's effects on the dependent variable.

So what is a researcher to do in order to ensure a successful study? Taking the potentially large denominator into consideration means emphasizing even more than usual the importance of a strong experimental treatment. In order for between-group variation to swamp within-group variance, the between-group effect needs to be substantial. Population-based experiments thus call for especially powerful treatments. To ensure a successful manipulation, the best single piece of advice is the same as what is given to any experimentalist: always pretest a manipulation before spending time and money collecting the data you care about. This point has been amply emphasized elsewhere (see any textbook on experimental design), so I will not belabor it here. But even with the limitations posed by population-based experiments, there are ways to enhance the prospects of an effective manipulation, as well as to gauge how much attention a treatment is actually receiving from respondents.

For purposes of encouraging effective experimental treatments in population-based experiments, below I outline six different considerations that can help improve the probability of a successful study. Only a few of these suggestions may be relevant to any given study, but either individually or collectively, they can make a difference in overcoming the obstacle of effective treatments.

Length and Processing of Treatment

By far the most problematic constraint in doing experiments remotely is the researcher's inability to know how much time and attention the participant devotes to the treatment. Population-based survey experiments do not allow the kind of close supervision of the research experience that laboratories do. We can ask a respondent to read ten screens of boring text in small font (in an Internet survey), or have the interviewer read a three-minute statement (over the telephone). But realistically subjects are probably not going to read or pay attention to anything of this length. Past a certain point, longer treatments seldom make more effective ones.

For this reason, the single most important factor in implementing effective manipulations is probably the length of the experimental treatment. If text extends beyond a single screen, the respondent must either scroll down the computer screen to read the rest of it, or hit a "next page" button in order to see the additional content. In our experience, expecting subjects to scroll down in order to see additional material was not a safe bet. Having the text on several screens was preferable, but the more screens of text they were asked to read without any questions to answer, the less likely participants were to carefully read and process the material.

Keep in mind that the amount that can fit on a single screen is quite limited. Treatments in population-based experiments sometimes consist of "articles" that participants are asked to read. Many investigators begin with the idea that they will have their stimulus look like a copy of a newspaper article, but then quickly discover why even online newspapers do not make their articles look like they do in a hard copy of the newspaper. The kind of formatting used in print publications is not necessarily the easiest to read on a computer screen. Ultimately, the font size and overall legibility of the treatment may be far more important to a study's success than whether it looks like a photocopy of a print article. If one incorporates participants who do not use personal computers (an increasingly small portion of the population), then font size is an especially important consideration. Of course, the bigger the font, the shorter the text that will fit on a screen.

The moral of the story is to keep manipulations short and to the point whenever possible, or be willing to risk less effective treatments. Moreover, those who come to this method from experimental disciplines need to remember that these are not all college-educated respondents. Some may find reading difficult, so the vocabulary and density should be geared to the audience to which newspapers are supposedly aimed: those with no more than an 8th grade education. In a telephone-administered survey experiment, the interviewer can be sure to read the entire manipulation, but she still cannot guarantee that the listener's attention will be held throughout, nor that he will comprehend all of the language.

If a manipulation must be text-intensive, then in addition to keeping it as readable as possible, another way to increase subject engagement is to intersperse the reading material with questions to answer, even if the answers to the questions are of little or no ultimate use to the researcher. People will read something if they think it is necessary to do so in order to answer a subsequent question. But when they read screen after screen of text and are not given any clear purpose for doing so, then participants may lack the motivation needed to ensure exposure to the treatment. The response format of most Internet surveys allows participants to speed through to the next screen, but this is much more difficult to accomplish when those pages include questions that need answering.[2]

Another means of increasing interest and involvement in experimental treatments is through the use of audio-visual materials. Still pictures, audio, and video are all currently possible as treatments via Internet, and most people find these materials more engaging than a page of raw text. Although researchers are not competing for Nielsen ratings, it is worth thinking in terms of competition for a participant's attention, which may be inherent to the environment in which people participate in population-based experiments. If participation in any given study truly is not all that interesting, then one may want to think about another kind of incentive to induce subjects to stay tuned in. It is generally a bad idea to ask respondents to do something outside the flow of the experimental session itself. For example, sending respondents to another website for their stimulus introduces immediate problems because the researcher is no longer assured that the respondent is actually exposed to the intended treatment.

Ideally, the researcher uses the techniques at his or her disposal to create an effective treatment. But for the sake of example, let us imagine that the subjects are not as cooperative as one might like in fully exposing themselves to the treatments. We can be certain they saw a given screen, but we know little about how much attention they paid to it. And perhaps a manipulation check suggests that not all respondents fully processed the treatment.

For post-hoc fixes, collecting information on the timing of individuals' answers to questions can be extremely useful on both telephone and Internet-based experiments. Interviewing software makes this process invisible to both the respondent and the interviewer, and it typically costs nothing extra to implement. Times are recorded between the keystrokes made by the respondent (in the case of self-administered interviews), or those made by the telephone interviewer who inputs answers into a CATI system (in the case of telephone interviews). After the experiment is executed, the investigator can decide on what is a reasonable length of time to progress from question to question and then look for extreme deviations.

For example, if one suspects that subjects may not have paid adequate attention to a manipulation, then extremely short screen times would be of greatest concern. In a multi-page text manipulation, if the first screen takes 20 seconds for a subject to read and process, but the third and fourth pages appear to have taken the same respondent only 5 seconds a piece, this should alert the investigator to a possible drop-off in close processing of the material. Respondents for whom time spent on the treatment

[2] Moreover, on an item-by-item basis, researchers can decide whether or not non-answering respondents should be probed and encouraged to answer.

screens appears too short—raising a potential concern about inadequate exposure—may be deemed suspect cases. Just as laboratory subjects may be dropped from a study with adequate reason (lack of cooperation, falling asleep on the job, guessing the purpose of the study, etc.), so too may participants in population-based experiments be dismissed if the justification is sufficiently convincing and systematically applied. However, if these "drop-outs" are non-random—that is, occurring more often in some conditions than others—then this approach can threaten the comparability of experimental groups.

Alternatively, if the "time stamp" indicating when the dependent variable was answered comes unusually long after the treatment exposure, then one might naturally be concerned about whether the treatment would still be influential, especially if it was intended to only momentarily alter something about the subsequent judgment. If an experiment is set up so that subjects may start it at one point in time, but finish it at another (substantially later) time, then the expected duration of the manipulation's effects also becomes a concern.[3] Those who take too long to answer may be distracted and/or the treatment may become so distant from the response variable that the anticipated effects are doubtful.

Given that response-timing data can be collected invisibly and automatically in either Internet or telephone surveys, there is really no good reason not to collect it. In light of the considerations outlined above, some researchers have ended up restricting their samples to those participants who spend a reasonable amount of time on the treatment and questions—that is, participants who took long enough to answer thoughtfully. For example, psychologists Eaton and Visser found much more consistent results in their experiment when the sample was restricted to those participants who took long enough to actually view the stimulus and thoughtfully answer the questions, but not so long that the effects of the priming manipulation wore off.[4]

Timing of Measurement and Persistence of Effects

An issue closely related to maximizing the power of the experimental treatment concerns *when* to assess the dependent variable relative to the treatment in order to maximize the anticipated impact of the treatment. The general advice in textbooks is to create treatments that are stronger than

---

[3] With Internet surveys, the investigator can choose whether or not to allow only those who complete the study in one sitting to remain in the sample, as well as whether they are allowed to use the "back" button to revert and change answers. This can be set up in advance at the investigator's discretion.

[4] See Eaton and Visser (2008).

you think you might need, because overkill is less risky than underkill. After all, an ineffective manipulation means that there is not much one can
do with a study. Toward that same end, many suggest keeping the treatment in close proximity to measurement of the dependent variable so the
treatment will not have a chance to "wear off" before the dependent variable is measured. This may be good advice in some cases, but there are
multiple considerations that should guide this decision.

One important factor to consider is what previous research using similar
manipulations has found to be adequate to induce a given independent
variable to change. If previous research suggests that your independent
variable is not easily manipulated, you should approach this issue differently than you would if multiple prior studies suggest that it can be done
with ease. If the latter is the case, then those previous studies probably also
provide models for how one might go about successfully manipulating the
independent variable, which could save you lots of pretesting and false
starts.

A second consideration is the anticipated persistence of the effect. Often
experiments are simulating one small effect that is expected to be tempo-
rary, but the treatment is expected to occur repeatedly over time in the
real world and thus persist due to replication rather than the longevity of
effects from a single treatment. Even an effect of short duration could produce a long-term impact if it occurs repeatedly over time. In these cases, it
is appropriate to assess the dependent variable soon after the treatment.
On the other hand, if the kind of change being induced is assumed to occur relatively infrequently, and the effect must be sustained over a period
of time in order to be of theoretical interest, then the longevity of a treatment's impact may be of greater concern.

If a given study is the first to establish some effect, it is probably best to
play it safe and minimize the time between treatment and outcome measures. However, if a potential concern and criticism is that such effects
would be too short-lived to matter in the real world, then a longer time
frame makes the most sense. Ideally, one measurement of the outcome
can occur when it is too soon for any effect to have worn off, and another
measurement of the same dependent variable can take place after a significant lag.[5]

There is still another consideration to take into account when deciding
on the spacing between treatment and measurement of the dependent
variable, and this concern occurs especially in the case of treatments designed to influence outcomes below a level of conscious awareness. Some
such manipulations—priming effects, for example—may be short-lived,
which suggests the need to measure the hypothesized outcome not long

[5] For an example of this approach, see Mutz (2005).

after treatment, or risk missing the effect entirely. On the other hand, the effectiveness of an experimental treatment may be undermined if it is so close to the outcome that it unintentionally implies a connection between the two. A noteworthy example of this takes place when emotions are intentionally manipulated, often by asking people about recent sad or happy events in their lives, in order to see how subsequent unrelated judgments are affected. In general, good moods produce more positive subsequent judgments and vice-versa for bad moods. But if people are told (or it is implied) that their feelings may be due to some irrelevant factor, then these effects are undermined.[6] By virtue of putting questions in close proximity to one another, the researcher may unintentionally imply a connection between them. Bringing a seemingly irrelevant connection to the participant's attention may actually undermine the effectiveness of the manipulation in this case, whereas greater distance between treatment and control would have strengthened it.[7]

Tailoring Treatments

In addition to being conscious of the factors that influence respondents' processing of a treatment, it is also possible to use background information to tailor treatments more closely to individual characteristics. At first blush, this may sound as if it violates the first principle of experimental design—that all people in a given experimental condition be treated exactly the same. But so long as the treatments and tailoring are applied according to the same systematic rules across all people in a given condition, tailoring will not confound the results, and it may well strengthen the experimental manipulation.

Tailoring can be used to operationalize a given treatment, or to strengthen an existing manipulation. In both cases the investigator must know information about the respondent in advance. For example, one population-based experiment incorporating the use of a tailored treatment did so in order to execute an experimental manipulation of similarity. All respondents were given advice on a judgment task by someone else, but in one condition it was someone who was described as highly similar to the respondent in their gender, geographic region, level of education, political affiliation, and age.[8] In the other condition, respondents were not given

---

[6] For example, Schwarz and Clore (1983) interviewed people on sunny or rainy days (a reliable effect on mood) and then primed people to think about the weather's impact on mood (or not). In general, mood affected judgments as one might expect, but when offered a reason for discounting mood as a source of information by calling it to attention, the impact was eliminated.

[7] See Malhotra, Healy, and Mo (2009) for a specific example.

[8] Gino, Shang, and Croson (2009).

any details on this "expert." Because demographic information of this kind had already been asked long in advance, the experiment could be programmed based on the answers that had already been given. So although people in the high similarity condition received different descriptions of the expert, in all cases within this condition, the experts were highly similar to the respondent.

In addition to allowing tailored operationalizations of concepts such as similarity, tailoring has been used to strengthen experimental treatments by utilizing advance knowledge of an individual respondent's vulnerabilities to manipulation. In this case, tailored treatments are typically "add-ons" rather than stand-alone treatments because not everyone in any given sample provides an opportunity for manipulation through a tailored approach. When random assignment is adhered to, and these vulnerabilities are not linked to the process of assigning people to conditions, the net effect is to increase the strength of the manipulation and the overall power of the experiment.

So, for example, in one study, I needed to systematically lower people's levels of generalized social trust in one experimental condition relative to the control condition. The treatment I chose for these purposes was a portion of a *Reader's Digest* article that highlighted disappointing results from an unsystematic "lost wallet" study conducted by the magazine.[9] Wallets containing money and identification cards from their owners were left in public places, and then observers watched as most of the finders pocketed the cash and made no effort to return the wallets or their contents to their rightful owners.

I certainly found it depressing to read. It seemed perhaps enough to convince my participants that people were generally untrustworthy, but I could not be sure. Moreover, a great deal of literature seemed to suggest that trust was not all that manipulable anyway, except perhaps over lifetimes or whole generations. Still other studies suggested that the experience of divorce generally lowers people's level of social trust, as does the experience of being a crime victim. These particular items caught my attention because I knew that members of the Web-based panels already had considerable information gathered on them, including whether they were divorced and whether they had been the victim of a crime.

Thus, in addition to the written stimulus designed to produce lower levels of social trust in all respondents in the low trust condition, I strengthened the manipulation by asking the divorcées who happened to be in this condition about their marital status (thus reminding them of their divorce). Likewise, those I already knew to have been crime victims were asked about whether they had had such an experience. Randomization

[9] Mutz (2005).

92

ensured that roughly equal numbers of crime victims and divorcees were in the low trust and control conditions, so that fact could not account for any observed differences. But being reminded of these experiences seemed to offer the potential for producing an even stronger manipulation—even lower levels of generalized social trust. Because considerable time passes between when a newly recruited Internet panelist answers a background question battery and when they might be included as an experimental subject (months or sometimes years), the chance of arousing suspicion in subjects by asking questions for which the answers are known is extremely small.

To review, the goal of a treatment is to manipulate the independent variable in the intended direction; the manipulation of the independent variable need not occur for the very same reasons nor even through the same process that it does in the real world in order for the manipulation to be valid. When treatments are criticized because, as is sometimes claimed, "That manipulation would never happen in the real world," this objection represents a misunderstanding, or at least considerable confusion, as to the purpose of an experimental treatment. The purpose of the study is not to simulate the process of real world change in the *independent* variable; the purpose is to see whether change in the independent variable (by whatever means) produces change in the dependent variable. So long as tailored treatments do not accidentally manipulate something other than the independent variable and create unnecessary noise, they can be of great help to researchers in achieving a potentially difficult manipulation. The more general point of the examples above is to take advantage of the large amount of background information available on Web-based panel respondents when it potentially benefits your research purpose. Determine what is already known about respondents that might aid the purpose of your research, and you may be pleasantly surprised.[10]

Within-subject Designs

In addition to tailoring experimental treatments based on advance knowledge of respondents, another method of strengthening population-based experimental designs is through within-subjects designs, which make it possible to observe the consequences of smaller, more nuanced treatment effects. By measuring the dependent variable twice for the same individual, and comparing the person to him- or herself at a later point in time,

---

[10] Although this will vary by company, health, economic, travel and political behaviors are likely to be available for many respondents. My personal favorite discovery was that a battery of questions on pet ownership (horse, dog, cat, hamster, ferret, etc.) was available for all of the National Annenberg Election Study Internet panel respondents (see Mutz, 2010).

the problem of large within-group variation is completely eliminated. All the variance left in the denominator is measurement error, so far more subtle manipulations and effect sizes will produce significant mean differences, even among a highly heterogeneous sample of subjects.

Although many researchers are aware of the strengths of this kind of design, it tends to be underutilized, perhaps because of the common fear that one might arouse suspicion by asking about the same dependent variable more than once in a relatively short period of time. But here, again, the structure of Web-based panels can be useful because they are set up with the assumption on the part of the company as well as the respondents that people will be repeat participants rather than one-time responders.

TESS used two different techniques to create a reasonable separation between repeated measures. Because of our role as aggregator of often unrelated studies, we occasionally had the opportunity to combine two different studies into a single interview module, so that the repeated measurements of the dependent variable would at least be separated by a chunk of time and a change of topic. Most Web-based interviews do not exceed 15 to 20 minutes unless they include additional incentives, so this approach is only practical within a single interview session when both studies are relatively short in duration. Even without TESS to combine studies, data collection companies may allot time within a single interview to more than one client, thus creating possibilities for some separation between repeated measurements. In the context of a single, limited time interview, the best solution for omnibus studies encompassing multiple experiments is to combine topics for which interactions seem highly unlikely.[11] This is obviously no guarantee, but an amalgamation of studies across many different disciplines makes this task considerably easier.

However, when this approach is not practical and/or there remain concerns about potential confounding, then Web surveys may be preferable because in this mode the attrition between multiple interviews with respondents is surprisingly low. Because of the ongoing nature of these respondents' participation, one can obtain a fairly accurate estimate of how many respondents one can expect to lose between a first and second inter-

---

[11] In the earliest cooperative efforts to allow population-based experiments to share time on a single telephone survey, many scholars were understandably concerned about the possibility that one investigator's experimental manipulation might interact with another investigator's treatment. The likelihood of confounding was compounded by the fact that many of the different modules combined in these early telephone surveys were on similar or closely related topics (see Gaines, Kuklinski, and Quirk, 2007). Although this is potentially a real problem when several studies are combined, so long as each study's randomization is carried out independently of every other study, this problem cannot result in a faulty inference of experimental main effects. The potential is in interactions among treatments and the investigators' ability to generalize findings outside of a potentially contaminated sample.

view in a repeated-measures design, and it is generally not so great so as to render impractical repeated measures across multiple interviews. The exact extent of attrition will depend on the nature of the sample as well as the length of time that elapses between interviews. But given the ongoing commitment of participants in Internet panels, multiple interviews and repeated-measures designs are surprisingly practical and efficient. This commitment also allows researchers to study experimental effects of potentially greater durations than the usual one-time laboratory treatment with immediate post-test.

Blocking

Beyond within-subjects designs, another underutilized strategy for reducing the size of the denominator in a population-based experiment is blocking. Blocking is used extensively in industrial experimentation, but for some reason it has been used far less often in the social sciences. Blocking only makes sense if the researcher has a good reason to believe that a given variable or characteristic will have a strong relationship with the dependent variable. So, for example, if one were studying the effects of a political message of some kind on attitudes toward increasing income taxes, and one believed that Republicans and Democrats would be likely to have quite different attitudes toward taxation, then one could block on political party.

In a blocked design, experimental subjects are first divided into homogeneous blocks *before* they are randomly assigned to a treatment group. So Republicans and Democrats would represent the homogenous blocks in the example above. Within each block, subjects would then be randomly assigned to the experimental conditions in predetermined (typically equal) proportions. Blocking shrinks error variance—that is, the variability that is not accounted for—though only so far as this particular variable is important to variance in the dependent variable. The randomized block design thus strengthens the power of the experimental design by reducing unwanted noise.

In an unblocked design, chance alone would seldom produce exactly the same number of Republicans and Democrats across conditions, while a blocked design can ensure an identical distribution of party identifiers in experimental groups. After all, randomization does not guarantee that all experimental conditions will be identical on all possible characteristics for any given randomization; it only suggests that this will be so across many randomizations. So in this example, if you do not want to risk ending up with conditions that are unequal and you want them to be truly identical with respect to political party in particular, then blocking is a good idea.

Internet-based studies can easily implement blocked designs because much is known about the respondents in advance (demographics and so forth) from an interview done when the respondent is first recruited to the panel. If the blocking characteristic (say, political party identification) is known in advance, then the flow of the experiment is set up to automatically condition on this variable. Even when scholars want to block on more complex concepts that have not already been asked in a previous interview, they can ask these questions before the randomization itself takes place during the flow of the study session. Given the ease with which this can be done, and the advantage of reducing an additional source of variability (in this example, the difference between Republicans and Democrats), why don't researchers block on lots of important sources of variability in the dependent variable?

As with the other techniques described above, blocking can reduce within-group variance and boost statistical power to identify significant effects. But there are trade-offs that suggest blocking is not always the best choice. First, blocking uses up degrees of freedom. Some blocked designs (such as paired comparisons) reduce considerably the number of degrees of freedom in the analysis. Others, such as factorial designs with a small number of conditions, use up fewer degrees of freedom (one less than the number of blocks). A blocked design with a small number of blocks will probably gain more power by blocking than it loses. One litmus test is to block if you expect the between-block variance to be greater than the within-block variance.[12]

Further, blocking is not a good idea if you care about the effect of your blocking variable, nor if you expect an interaction between your blocking variable and the treatment. If this is the case, you are better off using a factorial design in which both variables are manipulated independent of one another, as described in Chapter 4 and elsewhere. In the example above, party is obviously not easily manipulated experimentally, but some blocking variables are. If an interaction between block and treatment is expected, a factorial design should be used instead.

In practice, population-based experiments typically use difficult-to-manipulate, but highly influential factors for blocking. For example, in a study of how rising gas prices may affect health behaviors and gasoline consumption, Davis and Singer blocked on the presence of minor children in the home.[13] They hypothesized that families with minor children

---

[12] When the number of subjects is large, this is more conservative than is mathematically warranted, because a small amount of between-group variance will still be highly significant, but the advice is meant to take into account possible adverse effects of blocking on the robustness of the normality assumptions.
[13] Davis and Singer (2006).

would have different gas consumption patterns from those without kids. Given consistent family incomes, if gas prices go up and take up a larger proportion of people's disposable income, then expenditures on other things must decrease unless consumption of gas itself decreases. Families with children would have less elastic gasoline consumption, and thus they would be unlikely to make ends meet by reducing gas consumption than would people without minor children. Instead, people with minor children would be more likely to make ends meet by reducing spending on health care and consumer items.

Sample Size

One final issue worth further thought in population-based experiments is sample size. Of course, all investigators must consider sample size and statistical power in any experiment, whether conducted in the laboratory or elsewhere. But estimating required sample sizes via power analyses based on studies that have used small homogeneous samples may be misleading. The effect size anticipated based on previous studies may not be the same in the population as a whole, and the error variance is generally expected to be larger due to greater sample diversity.

Fortunately, the cost structure associated with population-based experiments typically means that investigators end up having much larger sample sizes than equivalent laboratory experiments. For example, the costs associated with programming a population-based experiment for a sample of 1000 people are not twice what they are for 500 people. The cost per interview goes down abruptly after the initial programming costs for a very small sample—a price structure that tends to encourage larger sample sizes. Most experimentalists would be thrilled with a 2 by 2 experiment involving 100 subjects per condition. But even so, the cost differential involved in shifting from a study with 400 respondents to 600 or even 800 respondents (and thus 200 people per condition!) is relatively small in a survey, so large sample sizes are quite common in population-based experiments. Moreover, it is typically easier to obtain a larger sample than to gather more data per person in a longer interview. People's attention spans and willingness to cooperate are limited, so longer studies typically require incentives that ratchet up the cost of the study as a whole.

Assuming you do have a larger sample than the typical laboratory experiment, this largesse can often be put toward useful ends. Most importantly, before launching your population-based experiment, *seriously consider the possibility of failure*. Assume that you successfully manipulated your independent variable, but it nonetheless does not produce the predicted effect on your dependent variable. What then? If there is some subgroup within the population as a whole that really should demonstrate the hypothesized effect if there is any truth at all to your theory, then who would those people be? And ideally how might you go about identifying them? Because of the larger sample size and more diverse population available in population-based studies, subgroup analyses can be highly productive.

Whoever the most susceptible are, make sure you have included the appropriate measures to identify them. That way, when the inevitable failure does occur, you will have a way to rescue your study from the potential obscurity of the file drawer. In reality, social science theories are seldom so universal as to apply to all people in all contexts. This is no reason to give up on a theory. Finding the boundaries of a given theory—the kind of people for whom it is true, as well as the people for whom it is not—is an extremely valuable contribution, and population-based experiments offer an excellent venue for doing this. Likewise, theories that work in one context may not work in another. People are (thankfully) complex and our theories often are not sufficiently complex.

Of course, some social scientists appreciate complexity more than others. One experimental study of mine that was under review at a major journal received interestingly mixed reviews based in this regard. The experiment was designed to test the hypothesis that exposure to politically disagreeable ideas could produce higher levels of political tolerance.[14] Given that observational evidence could only go so far in establishing the direction of this causal relationship, an experiment seemed the ideal next step, so I randomly assigned people to either receive lots of exposure to arguments they would find disagreeable, lots of exposure to politically agreeable arguments, or neither, and then measured political tolerance using a scale in standard use. I did not find a significant main effect for the main three-level factor. However, anticipating this possibility, I had also included an indicator of the personal characteristic that I thought should identify those most likely to demonstrate this effect, if anyone did. Using someone else's already-validated scale for perspective-taking ability, I hypothesized that people high in perspective-taking ability should be most likely to benefit in levels of political tolerance from exposure to oppositional views.

This interactive effect came through loud and clear. Nonetheless, one reviewer advocated rejecting the study because the experimental effect did not register in the sample as whole, only among this particular subgroup. At the same time, a second reviewer praised the subtlety of the hypothesis and said he/she found it much more convincing because it showed up precisely where it ought to—among those who actually listen seriously to others' views. The third reviewer largely concurred with this logic, sug-

14 See Mutz (2002).

gesting that the theory itself was hopelessly naïve, but it seemed entirely plausible within the constraints I had proposed and verified. In his/her view, the evidence was *more* convincing because it occurred only within these boundaries.

The important point here is simply to be prepared in order to maximize your publication opportunities. Regardless of whether one finds an across-the-board effect more or less convincing, there is no question that finding no significant effects at all would have been worse; it would mean that this study never saw the light of day. As researchers we cannot always get it right the first time, but usually we can still salvage the study and learn something important from it if enough forethought has been given to the prospect of limitations to theories. In short, the larger sample size of population-based experiments makes subgroup analyses feasible, so long as the investigator includes appropriate measures to identify these groups.

Moreover, even when a study works out as planned, and you obtain the effects you anticipate, it is still useful to have variables that identify the groups which, based on your theory, ought to be *most* susceptible to the experimental manipulation. Even if the main effect is significant, a significant interaction between the group and the treatment will help to build a stronger case for your particular explanation for this effect.

One final way to put all of those extra cases to work is by taking on multiple causal hypotheses at once. Some have suggested that population-based experiments are ill-suited to resolve issues of reciprocal causation.[15] However, by making use of control groups that serve double-duty, population-based experiments have been able to examine both potential causal directions efficiently within a single study. For example, in the social trust study mentioned earlier, the three conditions I described (low trust, high trust, and control) were really only three of the five conditions in the study. By manipulating levels of social trust, I wanted to see whether I could also change the likelihood that respondents would engage in online purchasing. Because the ongoing question in this area of research has been whether social trust alters economic behavior and/or economic behavior alters social trust, experiments are ideally suited to determine whether either, or both, of these processes is at work in creating this relationship. So the other two of the five experimental conditions manipulated online buying behavior by leading neophyte online shoppers to expect either positive or negative experiences when shopping online. Using a single control group for both hypotheses, this study established that causation was indeed flowing in both directions.[16]

---

[15] See Gaines, Kuklinski, and Quirk (2007).
[16] See Mutz (2005, 2009).

MEASUREMENT ISSUES IN POPULATION-BASED EXPERIMENTS

As described earlier in this chapter, the heterogeneity of random population samples can make it difficult to identify effects due to the relatively large amount of error variance. Some strategies for addressing this problem deal with increasing the size of the numerator in the F statistic (i.e., effect size), whereas others address reducing the size of the denominator (the variance that goes unaccounted for in the model). Yet another means of addressing this latter problem is simply paying close attention to measurement.

Because a study is an experiment, it is not necessary to include a huge number of potential "third variables" that might account for a spurious relationship between the independent and dependent variables; random assignment has already ruled those out. So for what purposes should we be using the rest of our survey interview time? I suggest that the best use of it is to improve measurement of the dependent variable. Perhaps because population-based experiments look superficially so much like surveys, investigators tend to rely on single item indicators, even for the most important of measures, the dependent variable.

Why are single item indicators so common in traditional survey research, even when everyone knows they are a bad idea? The answer is simply expense and the time constraints of the survey as a whole. Survey researchers need to fit in not only respectable measures of the independent and dependent variables of interest, but also as many potential spurious influences as possible. These additional variables are essential to making a strong causal argument in observational analyses, so scholars skimp on them at their own peril. But as I argue further in Chapter 7, including too many of these variables is unnecessary and potentially even harmful when analyzing experiments. In addition, surveys are often expected to serve as omnibus instruments attempting to cover a huge variety of topics for many different investigators all in one interview. Under these circumstances, it is at least understandable why so many studies rely on single item measures.

In a population-based experiment, however, there is no excuse for doing a poor job of measuring the dependent variable. Single item indicators are basically inexcusable in this context. Questions that might have been included in a survey for purposes of ruling out spuriousness can essentially be swapped for more thorough measurement of the dependent variable. The reason that investigators in population-based survey experiments rely on single item measures appears to be sheer force of habit leftover from survey research. The only way to know how well you are measuring your underlying concept is through the use of multiple items and assessments of reliability. When three or more closely-related items are combined into an index of some kind, they produce both an internal reliability estimate and a better measure of the underlying outcome of interest, one that is not as heavily affected by the peculiarities of any individual question. Ideally, the dependent measure should be based on more than the minimum number of items for assessing reliability. Keep in mind that the amount of "noise" in diverse population samples works against the ability to isolate effects, and thus more reliable and precise measurement is especially important in this type of study.

Are there exceptions to this admittedly strong admonition? Very few, though it is possible that previous research addressing measurement issues has established that a given item is the most valid and reliable way to measure a particular concept, and thus more extensive measurement efforts may be unnecessary. But seldom will this best possible measure be based on a single question.

Another scenario in which population-based experiments may focus on single item measures of questionable reliability and validity is when the study is focused on the issue of measurement and how to interpret evidence typically gathered through surveys. An excellent case in point is Holbrook and Krosnick's analysis of whether the usual self-report measures of whether people voted in an election are subject to social desirability pressures (see Chapter 2).[17] Experimental methods can be used to better understand what a longstanding single-item measure is tapping, and in this case measuring a behavior or concept sub-optimally is justifiable for purposes of better understanding the existing literature. In general, however, better measurement is essential for successful population-based experiments.

HOW DO I EXPLAIN A POPULATION-BASED EXPERIMENT TO MY IRB?

Many running the IRB gauntlet wonder whether they should tell their Human Subjects Committee that they are running a survey or an experiment. There is no correct answer to this question, but given the way IRB applications are often processed, the choice can have real consequences for how long the review process takes as well as for the level of scrutiny it receives. Surveys on all but highly sensitive topics are automatically exempt from IRB review at most universities, whereas all experiments are not. Experiments sometimes involve deception, which calls for a carefully worded debriefing at the end of the study, whereas surveys seldom include any explanations or debriefings.

---

[17] Holbrook and Krosnick (2004).

These statements are obviously generalizations, and federal rules for the protection of human subjects are implemented somewhat differently from place to place. Nonetheless, population-based experiments do not fit neatly into the categorization schemes that IRBs tend to use. Unfortunately, this can make the process of obtaining approval more rocky than usual, so allow a bit of extra time. My general advice to investigators has been to flag such a study as both survey and experiment, but to make sure that the experimental aspect of it is particularly prominent if there are any concerns about ethics or potential emotional or physical harm to subjects. Otherwise, treat it as you would a survey.

Increasing the strength of experimental treatments may run up against ethical constraints that are easier to surmount in the context of a laboratory experiment where investigators can debrief in person and obtain written consent from research participants, which is optimal from the IRB's perspective. But in actual practice, the differences between ethical concerns in a lab versus a population-based experiment are not all that great. The rules are the same and debriefing follows the same general form when called for, albeit with an online, electronic format.

Keep in mind that IRBs do not exist simply to restrict your research creativity and curtail what you can do with human subjects; they also protect us as investigators. If, for example, a human subject chooses to sue you because he or she is unhappy with your study for some reason, the university whose IRB approved your study will take care of all of the legal costs (do not ask me how I know this to be true). Your university lawyers will step in to take care of you, so long as you have played by the rules. And in any case, you have no choice.

Moreover, ethical norms are not solely about satisfying IRBs. Individual investigators may have personal norms that set a higher bar than the federal IRB rules or a given university's interpretation of them. Likewise, some disciplines have decided to adhere to their own internal norms. Most notably, economists have decided that, as a field, their experiments will not involve deception. The strength of this norm came as a surprise to me when I served as TESS Principal Investigator. One of the earliest studies we ran for an economist involved describing a scenario to participants that included a passive third party who received $5; in other words, this person did not actually do anything as part of the study and in reality did not exist, but the experiment described a person as having received this money. We had no problem with paying active participants based on their behavior in the game and had done so many times. But in this case, there was no actual person answering questions or participating in any way.

The economists insisted that we give away $5 for every person who heard this scenario as part of the study, so for a sample of just 500 people, that would mean distributing $2,500. I feared that our sponsor, the National

Science Foundation, might not understand, so I double-checked the advisability of doing this with their funds and received a green light. Editors of two economics journals confirmed that regardless of the study's results, it would only be publishable if we rewarded those imaginary people with $5 each. But then to whom should those funds go? The study investigators indicated that it needed to be 500 *different* people, exactly as implied by the separate statements made to each study participant, so donating it to a charity was out. I momentarily considered a party at a bar and buying drinks for everyone I knew in Philadelphia. Several of my graduate students volunteered to help. We also considered throwing Lincolns off the top of a tall building just for the thrill of it. But in the end, we chose the easiest route to randomly distributing cash and had it randomly given to people who participated in the Knowledge Networks panel, but not in this TESS study. It was not nearly as much fun as the other proposals, but it avoided any appearance of impropriety.

This whole episode caused me a great deal of cognitive dissonance because (a) I know how difficult research funds are to come by and how much time grant-writing takes, and (b) I could not see any way that giving away this money affected the integrity of this study nor subsequent ones. There are multiple rationales behind this norm, but some seem more compelling than others. No one argues that deception should be the first course of action when another would suffice, but I remain convinced that it is sometimes necessary and that strict adherence to a norm against it slows the accumulation of scientific knowledge. Even within their own field, economists disagree about whether and the extent to which the norm is beneficial. Interestingly, the arguments advanced in favor of this norm are almost exclusively methodological. The main arguments in favor of this prohibition are (1) that deception, even when it is not harmful to participants, hurts the quality of the experimenter-subject relationship and thus discourages research cooperation; and (2) that deception results in decreased naïveté on the part of experimental subjects, and thus less experimental control.[18] I probably would have been more sympathetic if the proscription had included a moral or ethical component, but that is not generally used as a selling point.

Importantly, if one focuses solely on the two arguments above, the prohibition does not apply equally well to population-based experiments. The first objection seems undeniably true when subjects are drawn from student subject pools; if deceived, those same subjects would be less likely to cooperate with the experimenter if invited back for another study.

---

[18] Although many economists have written on this topic, these two elements are summarized as the two central underlying objections in many discussions. See, e.g., Kelman (1967); Bonetti (1998); and Jamison, Karlan, and Schechter (2006).

However, the "quality of the experimenter-subject relationship" argument seems to suffer from a degree of hyperbole; given the short-term nature of most studies, few experimenters consider themselves to have much of a "relationship" to speak of with their subjects, even under the best of experimental conditions. A graduate or undergraduate research assistant has the most face-to-face contact with subjects in labs, but it is typically a very limited, one-time contact. Moreover, in population-based experiments, there is no contact whatsoever with the investigator, unless the participant requests such contact after the study is completed.

The second concern, decreased naïveté on the part of participants, strikes me as of greater consequence because it may affect the quality of a study's results. However, this problem stems from the repeated use of relatively small subject pools. When one depends on the same people over and over again for a series of experimental studies, deception is indeed problematic, as is the potentially increased sophistication of respondents. But this concern does not extend easily to population-based experiments. The pool of people available for population-based experiments is so large that it would be extremely rare to have the same person involved more than once. This renders concerns about repeat participation as well as the kind of "relationship" required to encourage participation moot. In Internet-based studies involving respondents who are empanelled for longer periods of time, repeat participation is possible. But only a small proportion of social science experiments require deception, and social scientific studies are a very small part of the (mostly marketing) research in which panel members engage. This means that the risks for population-based experiments are much lower than for laboratory studies involving relatively small subject pools.

Deception may seem on the surface to be a clear-cut issue; either subjects are lied to or they are not. But in reality it is often far more complex. Take, for example, a straightforward attempt at persuasion. Let us say that we tell subjects that Democrats do a much better job of handling the economy than Republicans do. Maybe we even add a bit of "evidence" to this persuasive appeal, citing the economic slide that began under a Republican presidential administration. If you are a Democrat, you are probably convinced that this argument is true, and thus perceive this treatment to require no debriefing. You are probably also not persuaded by it, because you already believed it to be true. If you are a Republican, you may call it deceptive or at the very least misleading information that should be accompanied by a debriefing if it is going to be used in an experiment.

But then one must construct wording for the debriefing, which often turns into a statement to the effect that, "The information you have been given may or may not be true." I leave it to your judgment as to whether such a statement is worth including. Most participants find it puzzling, to say the least. On the one hand, including this statement demonstrates honorable intentions on the part of the researcher, and if requested by investigators or their IRBs, we included such vague debriefings. On the other hand, I sincerely doubt that their inclusion changed any lingering effects that the treatment may have had.

Another way around this dilemma that has been used by many researchers is to preface treatments with statements to the effect that "Some people believe that . . ." But treatments of this kind inevitably manipulate more than they intend. To state that some people believe one thing is also to imply that others do not—that is, to imply that what follows is a controversial statement. Further, encasing the manipulation within the "some people" framework potentially invokes unintended social influence processes that vary in effectiveness across different segments of the population.[19] Unless social influence processes are of theoretical interest in the study, the manipulation may serve to muddy the waters of interpretation once a study's results are observed.

Demanding that experimental manipulations be verifiably truthful is a much higher standard than demanding that they not be outright lies. While the latter situation obviously demands a debriefing, the former is much less clear. The course of everyday life is full of false claims and potentially harmful consequences that may flow from accepting them. It is sad, but true, that the quality of information surrounding anyone who can access the Internet or watch television is far from this standard. Take, for example, the tremendously popular television program, *Oprah*. Oprah often invites people on her program to promote high-priced snake oil for everything from wrinkles to thyroid disease to cancer, and their claims typically go unchallenged and without debriefing.[20] Further, parents have been advised to eschew childhood vaccines for their children and to rely instead on positive thinking to cure what ails them.[21] We can only hope that our experimental subjects are not living in an environment in which they believe everything they are told.

One argument in response to the one I make above is that professors and universities hold a position of unique esteem in the American mind, prominence such that our questionable statements will be believed much more than something Oprah says. Don't we wish! Moreover, most Americans are regularly exposed to a tremendous amount of false and misleading information, and while I do not generally advocate spreading more

[19] See Mutz (1998).

[20] See Kosova and Wingert (2009).

[21] For example, as Kosova and Winger (2009) reported in *Newsweek*, Oprah promoted a product called The Secret: " "You're a field of energy in a larger field of energy," one of The Secret's teachers said. "And like attracts like, and that's very, very scientific." By harnessing this powerful science, they said, we can have anything we want—happiness, love, fabulous wealth."

of it, the use of deception must be understood in the context of risks and benefits, the holy grail of human subjects considerations. If a person is temporarily deceived for purposes of advancing scientific knowledge, it is more easily justified than if this is done for the sake of sensational television ratings.

In addition, the size of the pool of subjects must also be taken into account. Early in my career, I did an experiment using 105 undergraduates that was designed to alter their support for two local mayoral candidates—*if* my theory was (only partially) correct.[22] The design was balanced so that if it worked more than partially and pushed respondents in more than just one direction (as was anticipated), it would persuade as many people toward one candidate as toward the opposition, effectively canceling out its aggregate impact. The human subjects committee balked, arguing that my research might swing the outcome of the local election. Half of the committee was apparently convinced that my theory was wrong and thus was not particularly concerned about the study; the other half thought my theory was correct and might work, but nonetheless found the fact that it would have no aggregate impact on the outcome of the race insufficiently reassuring. The fact that no one knew whether the theory was correct made it obvious that I would produce a contribution to knowledge. And if history was any guide, this election would not be decided by as narrow a margin as 100 votes in any case. Eventually they relented, though not without controversy.

In short, there is much about everyday life that can potentially be unnerving or upsetting, or even misleading, and often social scientists want to study the effects of these phenomena. The question is whether this is an acceptable price to pay for the scientific knowledge that is being sought. The answer must depend on what the study is about. If participating in a social scientific study does not expose people to any greater deception or inaccuracy than does watching *Oprah* (an activity that is not generally considered harmful, even for children), then it seems reasonable to be open to the argument that the benefits outweigh the risks, particularly if debriefing is possible.

THE CHALLENGES OF IMPLEMENTATION

Population-based experiments are challenging to implement because the diversity of a randomly selected population makes it more difficult to identify the effects of experimental treatments. For this reason, it is important to consider a variety of different strategies to maximize the effectiveness

[22] Mutz (1992).

of the experimental treatments. First and foremost, manipulation checks are nearly always essential to establish that the experimental manipulation worked as intended in affecting the independent variable. Because investigators cannot directly verify participants' exposure to a stimulus as they can in a laboratory, manipulation checks are especially important to verify that the manipulation worked. Many population-based survey experiments neglect this important prerequisite.

Another means of improving the likelihood of identifying important results is through improvement of measurement. In particular, greater attention to the precision and reliability of measurement of the outcome variables can help toward this end by reducing unnecessary noise. Single item measures, which are common in survey research, are a particularly bad idea in population-based experiments. Moreover, given that "control" variables are not necessary for ruling out potentially spurious causes, such variables can and often should be sacrificed for more and better measures of the dependent variable. If the outcome measures are noisy, even a strong treatment effect can be difficult to observe. In Chapter 7, I discuss two final topics important to the successful use of population-based survey experiments: strategies for the statistical analysis and interpretation of results.

Analysis of Population-Based Survey Experiments

INVESTIGATORS TEND to approach the analysis and interpretation of population-based experiments from the perspective of usual practices in whatever their home discipline happens to be. Survey researchers analyze their data much as they would a survey, and experimentalists analyze them as they would any experiment. In many respects, this is harmless. However, as it turns out, some of these choices go hand in hand with common errors and faulty assumptions about the most appropriate way to analyze results from population-based experiments. Usual practices are not always appropriate, particularly with disciplines that favor observational methods. This chapter aims to provide guidance on best practices and to explain when and why they make a difference.

I proceed in roughly the order that these issues tend to arise in the data analysis process. I begin with the common practice of checking whether one's randomization has been successful after assigning subjects to experimental conditions. Next I discuss the issue of weighting data to known population parameters in order to increase generalizability. Finally, I focus on the use and misuse of covariates in the analysis and presentation of findings.

RANDOMIZATION CHECKS

It is common practice in many fields of social science to reassure readers that they can trust the internal validity of a given experiment's results by running so-called "randomization checks," that is, comparisons between various experimental groups on variables that are not part of the central theoretical framework of the study. Often these are demographics, but frequently they include other variables as well. The point of this exercise is supposedly to convince one's audience that this particular randomization did not happen to be one of those "unlucky" draws wherein some measured variable is unequal across conditions. By comparing means or percentages across conditions for a collection of variables, the investigator supports his or her assertion about the pre-treatment equivalence of experimental groups.

Unfortunately, this practice is problematic for several reasons. Although it is generally a mistake to do this in any kind of experimental study, this exercise has a tendency to get particularly out of hand in the case of population-based experiments. Perhaps because these studies produce a very large number of extra variables that come at no cost to the investigator, there is a temptation to run comparisons on a large number of them just to see if anything comes up significant. As I will explain, this is a statistically misguided idea in several respects. The problem is not the number of comparisons so much as the logical basis for doing them to begin with.

First, randomization checks demonstrate a fundamental misunderstanding of what random assignment does and does not accomplish. A well-executed random assignment to experimental conditions does not promise to make experimental groups equal on all possible dimensions. Across many independent randomizations this is likely to be the case, but not for any given randomization. Doesn't this pose problems for drawing strong causal inferences? Contrary to popular belief, it does not.

It is not necessary for experimental conditions to be identical in all possible respects, only on those characteristics that are potentially important to the outcome variable. Moreover, as sample sizes become progressively larger, the likelihood of chance differences across conditions becomes increasingly small. Given that population-based experiments tend to have much larger sample sizes and a larger number of subjects per experimental condition compared to laboratory experiments, there is even less cause for concern than with a traditional lab experiment.

But what should one conclude if one finds a difference in some characteristic that might be relevant? Doesn't that mean that the randomization essentially "failed"? When findings indicate no significant differences, the randomizations are claimed to be "successful," so this inference seems logical. But both assertions would be wrong or, at the very least, misguided. Psychologist Robert Abelson dubs this practice of testing for differences between experimental groups a "silly significance test."[1] As he explains, "Because the null hypothesis here is that the samples were randomly drawn from the same population, it is true by definition, and needs no data." Assuming there is no technical problem in the software that does random assignment, no systematic pattern in the random number table that is used, or some other concrete procedural glitch, random assignment is successful by definition so long as it is executed correctly.

Of course, if one does enough comparisons, one is bound to find a significant difference on one of them by chance alone. Given that population-based experiments often have as many as one hundred or more variables

---

[1] Abelson (1995, p. 76).

beyond the measures of the independent and dependent variables, a "failed" assignment is virtually guaranteed! Some scholars have suggested sensible statistical adjustments for combining multiple tests into one grand test.[2] These adjustments solve the problem of conducting too many tests, but they miss the larger point.

Although it is true that one can never totally eliminate the possibility of differences in experimental group composition, that probability has already been incorporated into the statistical tests used to test the null hypothesis of no differences between experimental groups. To reiterate, the infamous "$p < .05$" that tests the null hypothesis *already* includes the probability that randomization might have produced an unlikely result, even before the treatment was administered. So while there is no guarantee of avoiding a fluke result (short of replication, which should happen in any case), by conducting the standard test and reporting it correctly, researchers have already done due diligence.

Sometimes a population-based experiment is confused with a field experiment in which respondents may or may not have been exposed to the experimental treatment. If participants can opt out of, or select into, a given treatment group, then there is good reason for concern about non-comparable experimental groups. If for this reason treatment becomes correlated with some individual characteristic, it could easily confound the experimental results. In population-based survey experiments, respondents may opt out of taking a survey altogether, but they cannot opt into or out of a specific experimental condition; thus, noncompliance is not a threat to internal validity.

In general, a referee who suggests that an experiment requires a randomization check is probably well meaning, though wrong. Before a researcher succumbs to the temptation to "just do it" given that it will probably be insignificant anyway, he or she should consider what will happen if a difference does show up by chance. The most common "fix" applied in this situation is to try to "control" for any observed differences between conditions, much as one would with multivariate observational data. This well-intentioned practice is not only unnecessary, but also potentially counterproductive. Adding the "unbalanced" variable in an analysis of covariance does not remediate the situation, nor is the situation necessarily in need of remediation.[3]

To understand why, think about why this particular variable has been chosen for inclusion in the analysis to begin with; in this case, it is included strictly because of its significant relationship with the independent

---

[2] Hansen and Bowers (2008); Bowers (2010).

[3] As Senn (1994, p. 1716) notes: "The only reason to employ such a test must be to examine the process of randomization itself." See also Evans and Anastasio (1968).

variable. Thus when both variables are used simultaneously as predictors of the dependent variable, some of the variance in the dependent variable that would have been attributed to the experimental treatment will erroneously be attributed to the "control" variable instead, just as collinear variables in observational data may fight over the same variance in the dependent variable. Far from "fixing" anything, the investigator undermines the basis for unbiased experimental inference when including a covariate specifically for this reason.

I realize that the randomization check habit is a tough one to break. Many potential differences are arguably irrelevant because they have nothing to do with the dependent variable, so they will have little to no effect on the model.[4] But what about truly relevant group differences? Surely, one might argue, there are cases in which a difference between groups is so very central to the dependent variable that a difference across groups should not be ignored. Imagine that one were studying vote choice as the dependent variable, for example, but had experimental groups that differed significantly on party identification, a factor known to account for huge amounts of variance in vote choice. What should one do under these circumstances?

The real answer to this question is akin to what your parents tell you *after* your first automobile accident—that you should never have allowed yourself to get into this mess to begin with. Having already initiated the experiment and gathered the data, there is nothing much the researcher can do after the fact to correct for this problem without destroying the statistical integrity of the experiment. As described in the last section of this chapter, post hoc adjustments have the potential to make matters worse.

However, *before* the experiment is run, there is much one can do if there is a variable for which equality across groups is so very important that inequality on this characteristic would threaten the results of the entire experiment. With foresight one can engage in the experimental equivalent of defensive driving. One of two approaches can relatively easily eliminate this risk. The simplest approach is to hold the variable of concern constant among experimental participants. For example, if the purpose of the experiment on vote choice described above were to examine whether a light-skinned black Democratic candidate were judged more favorably than a dark-skinned black Democratic candidate, then it might be best to limit the sample to either all Democrats or all Republicans. By holding a highly important characteristic of the experimental groups constant, researchers avoid the possibility that the groups could end up dissimilar on this crucial characteristic by virtue of the limitations of randomization.

---

[4] See Thye (2007, p. 70).

But better yet, researchers could take an extremely important group characteristic and "block" on that variable, thus ensuring that there is no chance for the treatment groups to differ on that factor. The block then becomes another factor whose main effects are taken into account statistically. Although blocking is easy to accomplish in population-based designs, it is not without its own risks and drawbacks (as discussed in Chapter 6).

In short, "randomization checks" via significance testing can lead researchers down a misguided and fruitless path.[5] They are irrelevant to the internal validity of experimental results. Testing for demographic or other differences between experimental groups is misguided because a lack of differences on whatever variables happen to have been tested does not mean it was "successful" any more than finding a difference means that it was a "failure."

The only situation in which this type of check makes sense is when trying out a new randomization mechanism that may not be working properly. However, in this case, most researchers would have the foresight to try it out *before* the actual study was conducted. To be clear, my point is *not* to claim that random assignment always functions to make groups perfectly comparable because this is demonstrably not the case. However, this limitation is no justification for conducting randomization checks via tests of statistical significance. Some suggest that a legitimate rationale for doing so is psychological, rather than statistical: assuming the test indicates balance, it will increase readers' confidence in the findings. But if so, this is a misleading and false confidence; an insignificant randomization check has no bearing on whether imbalance actually matters to the experimental analyses.[6]

Weighting Experimental Data

Population-based experiments combine random assignment to treatments (to ensure internal validity) with random selection of observations (to improve external validity). Weighting is pertinent specifically to the latter concern: can we generalize a sample-based estimate of treatment effects to the population as a whole?

---

[5] This practice should not be confused with another common practice, that of providing a demographic overview of the experimental participants, so as to allow readers to judge the generalizability of the sample. This practice makes sense but serves an entirely different purpose from looking at demographics across experimental groups.
[6] See Pocock et al. (2002).

Although random probability samples are the highest quality obtainable in terms of representativeness, it is widely acknowledged by survey researchers that systematic differences exist in the ability to contact different kinds of people, as well as their willingness to cooperate. No one will argue that survey samples, however professionally obtained, are perfect these days; good response rates are increasingly difficult to obtain. Nonetheless, there is no question that these samples are still more representative than those obtained by any other method. The kind of external validity problems that stem from skewed and imperfectly representative survey samples can afflict population-based survey experiments as well, but the good news is that these problems can be dealt with in survey experiments as in surveys.

Probability samples of large populations are generally collected by professional survey organizations that deliver data along with a set of weights designed to make the sample more representative of known population parameters. Because non-response and other factors may skew the representativeness of a sample, weighting can be useful. In other words, well-executed surveys are very good, but not perfect, at incorporating all members of a population with equal probabilities.

Weighting can help with representativeness when descriptive accuracy is of concern, but only on the key variables that are used to produce the weights. Weighting requires known population parameters, so in the United States the characteristics used to create the weights are typically limited to basic characteristics known through the decennial census. When the population of interest is a subgroup for which population parameters remain unknown, weights cannot be calculated, and thus are not an issue.

Convenience samples cannot be weighted to produce accurate extrapolations to the general population. However, for samples that are close to being representative, weighting has been argued to be an effective tool for producing more descriptively accurate estimates of the population of interest. But when conducting a population-based experiment on a population with known parameters, what, if anything, should researchers do with these weights?

To my knowledge, there has been no systematic treatment of this topic to date, and some scholars have used weights while others have not. As a result, it is worth exploring at some length the potential promise and perils of weighting data to underlying population parameters. I begin this discussion by exploring the consequences of using the kinds of weights that are typically supplied by survey houses, that is, population weights that apply to the sample as a whole. In the subsequent section, I explore an alternative type of weight that might be used, one designed to make individual experimental conditions equally reflective of underlying population parameters. The good news is that either kind of weight can be used without biasing one's estimate of the treatment effect; however, as described below, considerations specific to an individual study can lead to different choices.

Weighting Whole Samples to Population Parameters

If estimation of the average treatment effect size for the population as a whole is a central purpose of a study, then weighting can be a useful tool toward that end. Assuming subjects are randomly selected from the population for whom the treatment effects are of interest *and* that population has known underlying population parameters, then weights offer the potential for more accurate estimation of the population average treatment effect. For simplicity's sake, I will illustrate this using a population with only one relevant characteristic potentially used for weighting, say gender, and a simple two condition design with treatment and control groups.

The first issue to consider is homogeneity of treatment effects. In this and any other study, if all subgroups are affected equally by the treatment, then the representativeness of the sample is of no concern in correctly estimating the size of the average population treatment effect. There are four relevant means of the dependent variable, *Y*, as illustrated in Table 7.1. Men and women may start out in different places and have different means for treatment and control conditions, but, if they are all affected to an equal extent by the treatment as in this example (that is, there is no *interaction* between gender and treatment), then weighting is irrelevant and will not change the estimated effect.

But given that investigators may not know in advance whether effects are homogeneous, the possibility of heterogeneous effects (as shown in Table 7.2) needs to be taken into consideration. In Table 7.2, women are far more susceptible to treatment effects than are men.

Because of random assignment to conditions, it is possible to correctly assess the average treatment effect in a sample population even with het-

TABLE 7.1.
HOMOGENEITY OF TREATMENT EFFECTS AMONG MALES AND FEMALES

Means by Cell	Control	Treatment	Effect Size
Male	0	3	+3
Female	6	9	+3
Sample Average	3	6	+3

TABLE 7.2.

HETEROGENEITY OF TREATMENT EFFECTS AMONG MALES AND FEMALES

Means by Cell	Control	Treatment	Effect Size
Male	0	3	+3
Female	6	15	+9
Sample Average	3	9	+6

Note: Table 7.2 assumes equal numbers of men and women in the population and in the sample, and equal numbers of control and treatment respondents in the sample.

erogeneous effects. In the example above, for males, treatment increases the mean by 3, whereas for females it increases the mean by 9 units. If there are equal proportions of male and female subjects in the population and in the conditions shown above, then the sample average treatment effect is 6.

But if the treatment effect differs across subgroups and the sample *does not* have precisely the correct composition by subgroups relative to the general population, then one will inaccurately generalize from these results to produce an estimate of the population average treatment effect. For example, if there are too many women, the estimate of average effect size in the population will be too large, and if there are too few women, it will be too small.

Can weighting help with situations of this kind? If sample selection bias interacts with treatment—that is, the cooperators in the survey sample respond differently to treatment than the non-cooperators—then there is nothing one can do to provide a "fix" for the problem. No amount of weighting nor any other fancy statistical manipulation will correct the erroneous sample-based estimate of treatment effects. This may sound like a severe limitation, but it is worth keeping in mind that this same assumption is also implicit in survey weighting more generally. Extrapolation from those who are interviewed to those who have not been interviewed only makes sense if study participation is unrelated to the outcome of interest.

If those who cooperate and those who do not can be assumed to be affected similarly by the treatment, then weighting is feasible. For example, what happens if we weight subjects to equalize the sample population with the general population with regard to gender? Assume that men and women are equally prevalent in the general population, but that in a sample of 120 people, data are gathered on 40 men and 80 women due to a 50%

rate of non-cooperation among men as opposed to perfect cooperation among women.

Suppose that the randomization into treatment and control conditions splits the two subpopulations equally into control and treatment groups. In other words, as illustrated in Table 7.3, there are 20 control males, 20 treatment males, 40 control females, and 40 treatment females. Assuming that cooperation does not influence the size of the treatment effect, the mean of Y in the control group in the sample should be 0 as it was in Table 7.2. Applying the effect sizes in Table 7.2 to all four means and averaging shows that the mean of Y over the control group (males and females) should be 4, while the mean of Y over the treatment group should be 11; the unweighted estimator for the treatment effect is the difference, which is 7.

However, by weighting the sample to accurately reflect the underlying 50/50 split between men and women that we are assuming in the general population, we can reclaim the correct population average treatment effect. Ideally the sample should have been 120 people in which 60 were men and 60 were women. Weights achieve this by giving each male a weight of 1.5, and each female a weight of .75. After weighting, the weighted cell counts become 30 per cell and 60 per condition. The new treatment mean in the sample is 9, and the new weighted control mean is 3. Thus, the aver-

TABLE 7.3.

HETEROGENEITY OF TREATMENT EFFECTS WITH DISPROPORTIONATE
NUMBERS OF MALES AND FEMALES

Means (Counts by Cell)	Control	Treatment	Total
Male	(20)	(20)	(40)
Female	(40)	(40)	(80)
Total	(60)	(60)	(120)
Column Mean Effect Size	4	11	+7

Note: Hypothetical cell counts for each cell are indicated in parentheses. The means that one would obtain for each column, assuming effect sizes as indicated in Table 7.2, are calculated by taking the disproportionate counts in Table 7.3, multiplying them by the effect sizes in Table 7.2, and then dividing by the column sample size. For example, for the control group, $(20(0) + 40(6))/60 = 4$.

age treatment effect is 6, and we have recovered an unbiased estimate of the mean treatment effect in the full population.

In short, when randomization serendipitously equalizes the number of treatment and control subjects in the relevant subgroups *and* it can be assumed that cooperative and non-cooperative members of any given group would be similarly affected by the treatment, then weighting has the potential to completely correct for uneven group sizes. Unfortunately, random assignment seldom perfectly equalizes the size of the relevant subgroups across experimental and control conditions.

So suppose instead that the 60 people chosen as controls happen to contain 10 males and 50 females, as shown in Table 7.4 below, whereas the 60 chosen for treatment have 30 males and 30 females. These proportions would be very unlikely if the sample size were much larger, but they are not completely out of the question in a sample size of 120. Table 7.4 gives the unweighted cell counts (on the left) and then the counts weighted to reflect the known population parameters (on the right) for a population evenly split between males and females, with a sample size of 120, and 60 respondents per condition.

Using the weighted data, and assuming the same underlying effect sizes as shown in Table 7.2, the weighted control group mean comes out to be $\bar{Y} = 4.28$ (computed as $(15(0) + 37.5(6))/52.5)$, while the weighted treatment group mean is $\bar{Y} = 7.00$ (computed as $(45(3) + 22.5(15))/67.5)$, leading to an estimate for the mean treatment effect of 2.72. This estimate is wildly incorrect. The problem occurs because males were more likely to be in the treatment group simply by chance. Male scores are systematically lower in all conditions, so this depresses the estimate of treatment effect size. This example illustrates the potential perils of weighting to population parameters.

Without any correction, we would compute the mean of the dependent variable in the treatment group to be 9 (computed as $(30(3) + 30(15))/60$), and the mean in the control group to be 5 (computed as $(10(0) + 50(6))/60$). The difference of 4 is too low an estimate of the mean treatment effect in the population, but it is not as bad as the "corrected" estimate using weights. The use of weights is intended to fix the problem of generalizability to the full population, but in the unlucky case in which two subpopulations are different, and randomization does not create equal cell sizes (as in the accidental correlation between treatment and gender above), weighting can cause estimates to go further awry.

The possibility of an uneven randomization is always present, but it can be avoided in one of several ways if one anticipates heterogeneous effects by demographic subgroups. The simplest is to block on gender—or whatever the subgroups of interest are—in the design stage. As described in Chapter 6, blocking means forcing the subgroups to be equal across

TABLE 7.4.
COMPARISON OF WEIGHTED AND UNWEIGHTED CELL COUNTS

(Counts)	Unweighted Cell Counts			(Counts)	Weighted Cell Counts		
	Control	Treatment	Total		Control	Treatment	Total
Male	(10)	(30)	(40)	Male	(15)	(45)	(60)
Female	(50)	(30)	(80)	Female	(37.5)	(22.5)	(60)
Total	(60)	(60)	(120)	Weighted Totals	(52.5)	(67.5)	(120)

Note: The unweighted cell counts on the left are given as hypotheticals; the weighted cell counts on the right demonstrate what happens when the unweighted counts are weighted to reflect an underlying 50/50 distribution of males and females in the population in a sample of size 120. So, for example, to produce 50% males in a sample of 120, the 40 existing males must be weighted by 1.5 in order to produce 60 weighted males. The 80 females must be weighted by .75 in order to equal 60, and so forth.

control and treatment conditions. For example, in this case the 40 men would be equally split between treatment and control, and likewise with the subgroup of 80 women. In other words, the investigator forces the cell counts of an "ideal randomization."

Alternatively, when heterogeneity of effects occurs along with sample subgroups that are under-represented or over-represented in the sample, it is possible to analyze the two subpopulations separately, estimating the treatment effect separately within each subgroup and using the known target proportions to extrapolate effect sizes to the full population. This is most effective when there is relatively little measurement error in categorizing subjects by subgroup, as is the case with gender- or age-based subgroups.[7] Another way one might reduce the noise of uneven randomization is to include in the model both gender and an interaction term between gender and treatment. In the simple 2 by 2 case discussed above, this is mathematically equivalent to separating the two sub-populations.

For the sake of simplicity, the examples above concerned weighting along a single dimension. More commonly, weights are available along a small set of population parameters, such as age, gender, race, and urban/rural area of residence. The sample may be weighted to match census data, not only for the marginals of these characteristics but in a cross-tabulated manner, thereby obtaining the correct weight for each category (e.g., white, female city dwellers between 40 and 59 years old). When available, these weights are superior as they more closely capture characteristics of the full population.

To summarize, weighting the sample as a whole to known population parameters will not bias the inferences that are drawn from experimental findings. If one expects significant heterogeneity of effects on one of the variables used for weighting, then blocking should be used at the design stage, or another kind of weighting should be considered, as described below.

Weighting Experimental Conditions to Population Parameters

Beyond the options of (1) not using weights at all, and (2) weighting the sample as a whole to underlying population parameters, a third option is to use weights that are formulated so that each individual experimental condition reflects the population parameters. To extend the example above, in this case the weighting scheme would be designed to produce the correct proportions of men and women within each of the two experimental conditions, not just in the sample as a whole. In our example in the left

---

[7] For a discussion of extrapolation when the population is separated along lines that are inferred, see Druckman and Kam (2010).

panel of Table 7.4, with counts 10, 30, 50 and 30, the desired sample counts mirroring a full population that is half male and half female would be 30 per condition. In the control group, therefore, we would weight males by 3 and females by .60, while in the treatment group we would weight males by 1 and females by 1. These weights, shown in the left panel of Table 7.5, create the ideal cell counts (all equal to 30) as shown on the right-hand panel of Table 7.5. Further, when combined with the effect sizes originally shown in Table 7.2, the separately weighted conditions produce the correct full population treatment effect equal to 6, as shown on the right panel in Table 7.5.

In this example, within-condition weighting worked very well; it produced an unbiased estimate of the average treatment effect in the full population with very little noise. Is within-condition weighting thus generally superior to using the usual full sample weights? Unfortunately, there has been little exploration of these issues to date. The practice of weighting was developed as a survey research tool—that is, for use in observational settings. The use of experimental methodology with representative samples is not yet sufficiently common for the analogous issues to have been explored in the statistical literature. Either weighting scheme has the benefit of increasing generalizability to the full population. However, as shown in the examples above, the side benefit of reducing noise due to uneven randomization is obtained through within-condition weighting as illustrated in Table 7.5, but not generally through full sample weighting, as shown in Table 7.4.

The reason one approach is not clearly superior to the other is because of the downside that exists to all forms of weighting. Although weighting subtracts some noise, it adds other noise, and thus can reduce statistical power. Consider a situation in which the investigator has both kinds of weights at his or her disposal. If all the full sample weights are squared for a sample of size n, and then summed across all subjects, this sum (call it M_1) provides a sense of just how much power is lost through weighting:

$$= 1 - \frac{n}{M_1}$$

If all sample weights are 1 (and thus there really is not any need for weighting), then M_1 will be equal to the sample size, and our estimate of lost power will equal 0. On the other hand, if $M_1 = 3000$ and $n = 2000$, then the equation above will come out to .33. This can be interpreted to mean that weighting in this case increases the extent of noise and lowers statistical power as if we had reduced the sample size by one-third. Instead of a sample of 2000, we effectively have the power of a sample size of 1340.

TABLE 7.5.
ESTIMATED TREATMENT EFFECTS WHEN WEIGHTING *WITHIN* EXPERIMENTAL CONDITIONS

Within Condition Weighting				*Effect Estimates After Weighting Within Condition*			
Means (Counts) [Weights]	*Control*	*Treatment*		*Means (Counts)*	*Control*	*Treatment*	*Effect Size*
Male	(10) [3]	(30) [1]		Male	0 (30)	3 (30)	+1.5
Female	(50) [.6]	(30) [1]		Female	6 (30)	15 (30)	+10.5
				Sample Average	3	9	6

Note: Entries are means by cell with cell counts shown in parentheses and weights shown in brackets.

If we were to calculate M_2, the sum of the squared deviations for within-sample weights in the same hypothetical study above, then M_2 will generally be greater than M_1; assuming the same total sample size, there will be greater unevenness in representing the population in the individual experimental conditions than in the study as a whole, thus necessitating larger weights. This means that the sacrifice in power will also be greater than with a full sample weighting scheme. Noise will be greater for within-condition weights than for full-sample weights. This must be balanced against the advantage of within-condition weights. The relative difference in power can be calculated by M_1/M_2. The only way in which within-condition weighting is inferior to full-sample weighting is in the potential for M_2 to be large.

The same caveats apply to either type of weighting. Weighting will lead researchers astray if there are interactions between selection and treatment effects. Beyond these caveats, inferences derived from within-condition weighting are as valid as inferences derived from the more traditional weighting scheme. In particular, the estimate of the treatment effect will be unbiased. A quick computation of the sum of the squares of the two different kinds of weights will make it clear whether the researcher has lost significant power by using weights, and whether the difference between the extent of power loss using the two strategies is negligible or not.

Whether the sacrifice in power from using weights is worth it or not in order to achieve greater generalizability is a question that must be answered in the context of each individual study. If it is a well-established experimental finding and the main purpose of the study is to estimate the size of the population average treatment effect, then it may well be worth it. On the other hand, if the anticipated effect is small in magnitude and statistical power is important in identifying the mere existence of the effect, then weighting might not be of the utmost importance.

If an investigator plans to use weights, then he or she should find out which respondent characteristics are used for weighting and decide whether or not those specific dimensions have implications for what he or she is studying. If the characteristics used for calculating weights do not have implications for the size of treatment effects, then weighting is probably a non-issue for this particular study. If they are potentially important, consider blocking on this characteristic. If blocking is not possible or desirable for some reason, then ask for both types of weights. Whereas survey houses nearly always supply full-sample weights as a matter of course, when executing population-based experiments they should be asked to supply within-condition weights as well.

The decision of whether and how to weight boils down to thinking about heterogeneity of effects, specifically with respect to the characteristics available for use in weighting. This latter limitation makes the decision far less complex than it would otherwise be. I am a firm believer that most treatment effects are heterogeneous on some dimension; it is difficult to find a social science theory so universal that it works to the same extent on all people in all contexts. On the other hand, weights are only possible for a few limited dimensions of the sample, so the likelihood that a given treatment's effect is heterogeneous specifically with respect to one of those dimensions is much less likely. If experimental effects are expected to be heterogeneous by some subgroup for which accurate population parameters are known, then weighting on population characteristics is advisable if one hopes to accurately estimate population average treatment effects. If effects are known or expected to be heterogeneous by some group characteristic, but the sample is roughly representative on that characteristic, then weighting in general (and its consequent loss of power) is not worth it.

USE OF COVARIATES

A third issue that arises in the analysis of population-based experiments is the appropriate use of covariates. Investigators from experimental traditions and survey traditions tend to approach this issue very differently. Those coming to population-based experiments from the survey tradition tend to analyze experiments in the same way that they would observational data; that is, they run a large regression equation including many demographics and other "control" variables thrown into the mix. There is good reason for this when analyzing observational data. Making a strong causal argument rests on establishing (1) temporal precedence of the independent variable, (2) an empirical relationship between the independent and dependent variables, and (3) the lack of any spurious correlation. Control variables are necessary (though, alas, not sufficient) to rule out spurious relationships in observational studies.

Those trained in the experimental tradition, however, rarely build large-scale regression models to analyze their data. As I will argue, few population-based experiments actually benefit from such an approach. Because of the experimental protocol, temporal precedence and spurious correlation are not issues (other than the small probability of a random spurious correlation, quantified by the p-value). A significant empirical relationship between independent and dependent variables all but guarantees causal inference.

In this case the utility of covariates is limited to their ability to reduce noise, thereby increasing the chance that the empirical relationship reaches statistical significance. When it comes to covariates, the good news is that analyses provide valid estimates and inferences about experimental effects even when the model is not correctly specified.[8] For some scholars, this has served as a rationale for throwing everything but the kitchen sink into their models. What scholars tend to misunderstand is that covariates are not always helpful or even benign influences. To haphazardly include a long list of covariates in your analysis of variance, or throw a batch of additional variables into your regression is not wise.

To understand why, and under what circumstances it makes sense to include a covariate, it is helpful to think about what happens in a statistical computation when covariates are included: the dependent variable is replaced by a value adjusted for the effects of the covariates. Ideally, these adjustments would be without error, but in reality, the estimates for covariates must be estimated from the data. The statistical analysis is then run with these adjusted values in place of the original values. To the extent that the covariates actually predict the dependent variable, the adjusted values should have less variance; estimates of the treatment effect should be more precise and the ratio of between-group variance to within-group variance should be higher because the denominator is smaller. However, to the extent that the estimates of covariate impact deviate from their true values, the adjustments will reflect noise and add a meaningless (though unbiased) quantity to the values of the dependent variable used in the subsequent analysis. The within-group variance will appear not to have grown, but the critical value is now actually greater, as manifested by the change in the number of degrees of freedom. In this case, the accuracy of the estimate of the treatment effect is reduced.

In order to choose wisely, one would like to be able to compare these two effects: gain of power through reduction of variance, and loss of power due to random error in the estimation of effects from covariates. This is not so easy. We have only a noisy estimate of how much has been gained (the amount of variance in the dependent variable explained by the covariates), and only indirect ways to guess how much noise the covariates might be adding. When a covariate clearly explains some reasonable fraction of the variance in the dependent variable, it usually appears to be helpful to include it. But what is a reasonable guideline? The threshold at which the gain in reduced within-group variance is smaller than the loss due to one less degree of freedom is probably too complicated to compute except in a very simplified model, and thus provides little guidance.

Here one must rely on theory and previous empirical research. If there is a compelling theoretical argument that a covariate will predict the dependent variable well, then include it; it is very likely that the predictive

---

[8] In particular, no assumptions of linear relationships with the dependent variables, normality, or lack of interaction are needed for unbiased estimation, with or without covariates. For a general discussion, see Freedman (2008).

power of the covariate will exceed the threshold where it is a help rather than a hindrance. But it is not acceptable to go "fishing" in the data set itself for strong covariates. For valid statistical inference, one should decide on covariates before analyzing the data. A strong theoretical and/or empirical argument provides convincing evidence that the decision was made *a priori*.

Still, in order to answer the question of whether a relationship is strong enough that the likely gain from correction exceeds the loss from added noise, some quantitative guidelines are useful. One helpful guideline suggests that for a single covariate, the gain in power is the ratio of the variance of the dependent variable to the adjusted variance. The loss of power due to noise is likely to be a factor of $1 + r^2$, where r is the standardized covariance between the covariate and the treatment variable.[9] Due to randomization, this is usually quite small: its magnitude is inversely proportional to the sample size. Therefore, we might begin by saying that with a subject pool of 500 respondents, we should include covariates for which there are theoretical reasons for believing that they should explain at least about half a percent of the variance in the dependent variable. However, one must be wary of diminishing returns. If many covariates are included, they all compete to explain overlapping sources of noise in the dependent variable, and the marginal explanatory power of any one covariate will be much less than if it were the only covariate in the model. This is particularly true if there is high collinearity among the covariates, though it is not limited to this case.

With population-based experiments, typically there are many potential covariates. It is not uncommon for the delivered data to include a demographic battery with 30 to 50 items. This increases the opportunity to sharpen an analysis by including covariates, but it also increases the possibility for diminishing returns and loss of power through degrees of freedom. This is particularly likely to be problematic if you are also including interaction terms or if some of the covariates are categorical with many categories. The more covariates that are thrown into a model without theoretical rationale, the more likely this is to happen.

One final reason to limit the use of covariates is transparency. The beauty of experimental design is that the presentation of results is clear and easy to interpret. When, instead of a set of means for the dependent variable, one presents a version of the outcome that has been adjusted for a large set of covariates in a complex model, one loses that simplicity. Readers' attention is distracted from the central result and focused instead on acceptance of the model as a whole. Needless complexity seldom makes for better experimental research.

---

[9] This guideline can be found in Franklin (1991).

The surest way to achieve a significant result if there is a variable expected to strongly influence the outcome is to block on that variable, which completely eliminates the portion of the noise predicted by the blocking variable. There is no reason to include a covariate, *post hoc*, unless the researcher had a reason to include it before discovering the relation with the treatment variable.[10] A practical rule of thumb is to include one or two covariates if you have a clear reason for believing they will substantially predict the dependent variable. Remember that experimental inference is always valid with no covariates whatsoever. But just one or two covariates should suffice to reduce the within-group variance enough to observe the hypothesized effect.[11]

AN EMBARRASSMENT OF RICHES

A central advantage of experiments is that analysis is typically simpler and more elegant than for observational data. However, population-based experiments come with an embarrassment of riches when it comes to additional variables. This surplus leaves many analysis decisions up to the investigator. Unfortunately, the excess of data often leads analysts toward some common mistakes.

These additional variables can be used (and misused) toward a variety of ends. As I have discussed in this chapter, one common use for these variables is to check for baseline comparability across treatment groups, and possibly "adjust" for these differences. This practice is simply misguided. The statistical significance of a randomization check has no bearing on whether the imbalance matters to the analyses.[12] Unless one suspects a technical problem, this practice is philosophically and statistically unsound, of no practical value, and potentially misleading. If a randomization "fails" such a check, there is nothing one can or should do about this. Including a control variable because of a "failed" randomization check does not adjust for the problem and only makes matter worse. Randomization checks reflect a lack of confidence in the power of random assignment to equalize measured and unmeasured variables across conditions, as well as a misunderstanding of what statistical tests take into account.

---

[10] In quasi-experimental designs, by contrast, the practice of including nearly everything is quite defensible. Quasi-experiments are deemed "quasi" precisely because they do not have control over random assignment. In this case, there is no reason to assume up front that the treatment and third variable are orthogonal and a common way to establish causal inference is to throw in everything.

[11] For a more quantitative discussion, see Tsiatis et al. (2007) or Mutz and Pemantle (2011).

[12] As Pocock et al. (2002, p. 2928) summarize, "P-values for baseline differences do not serve a useful purpose since they are not testing a useful scientific hypothesis."

Survey data are often accompanied by sample weights, thus offering the possibility of still greater generalizability of the survey experimental sample. Deciding which weighting schemes make the most sense in any given study depends on the purpose of the study and the nature of the treatment's anticipated effects. Such corrections can be important when calculating an accurate estimation of a treatment effect, particularly if there are interactions between the treatment and the demographic variables used in weighting.

Third, covariates tend to be overused in the analysis of population-based experiments. While potentially useful in increasing the efficiency of an analysis, covariates can also decrease power, so they should not be thrown into models haphazardly as if without consequence. In this case, for the reasons detailed above, they should be chosen with forethought, and both adjusted and unadjusted means should be presented to readers. A lack of clear guidelines for the inclusion of covariates has led to their overuse in analyzing population-based experiments.

More generally, decisions about experimental design and model selection are meant to be made before data collection. Post-hoc selection of covariates out of a larger set of potential covariates can lead to biased estimates of the treatment effect,[13] although this problem is less consequential with large samples. A large sample size is the functional equivalent of multiple randomizations; over many randomizations and/or a large enough sample, the potential for covariates to vary by experimental condition becomes asymptotically small.

This standard of pre-defined statistical models is nearly impossible to enforce. Nonetheless, the error estimates and confidence statements produced by most statistical software assume this normative protocol. It is for this reason that reviewers can and should ask serious questions about why certain variables are included in any given model. Without a strong, convincing justification, there is reason to suspect that data dredging may be afoot. Investigators are generally better served by relying on the simplicity and elegance of the experimental design rather than formulating highly complex multivariate models. Randomization checks and equations chock full of "control" variables reflect a fundamental misunderstanding of how experiments work. Random assignment to conditions means that the very notion of "control" variables makes no sense because control is already embedded in the design itself.

Finally, I will add that in presentation as well as in analyses, investigators should present findings in as transparent and straightforward a manner as possible. For example, if an experimental design involves a 3 by 2 factorial design including interactions, then it makes little sense to present

---

[13] See Pocock et al. (2002).

a complex regression equation full of dummy variables and their many interactions when a straightforward analysis of variance and a table of means would be far easier to interpret. Although this choice will not affect the results in any way, it can easily affect readers' understanding of results when they are presented in a more complex fashion than need be.

In my own field, the "obsession with regression"[14] as the one and only means of analyzing data produces some oddly complex presentations of relatively simple and straightforward findings. I have nothing against regression, but it is not the only tool for analysis. Often an analysis of variance along with a display of means makes a far simpler and more understandable presentation, particularly when interactions are involved. The real beauty of experimental results is that they are simple and do not require sophisticated statistical estimation methods nor long equations to understand. As a result, experimental findings can be easily communicated even to a lay person. In this case, the lack of complex statistical methods is a sign of the strength of the design itself, and the transparency of the results only contributes to the persuasiveness of findings.

In short, population-based experiments are accompanied by an embarrassment of riches that can both aid and impede research progress. The key to making this method profitable for social scientists is to make wise choices about experimental design and what to do with these data once collected.

---

[14] Firebaugh (2008, p. 209) suggests that this obsession unfortunately afflicts many fields of social science.

PART III

SITUATING POPULATION-BASED SURVEY EXPERIMENTS

External Validity Reconsidered

To DATE, THE MAIN rationale for promoting population-based survey experiments has been external validity. In reflecting on this claim, it became clear to me that things were not so simple as that for several reasons. First, not only was generalizability itself poorly defined, but the received wisdom regarding the generalizability of existing research designs was also highly questionable. In order to sort through the truth and fiction behind these claims and identify the advantages of population-based survey experiments, I begin with a reassessment of the usual heuristics for assessing both internal and external validity.

As social scientists, most of us somewhere early in our training encountered the well-worn maxim that internal validity is fundamentally at odds with external validity. We are told that there is an inherent tension between the two, such that an increase in one form of validity must come at the expense of the other. Experiments maximize internal validity through random assignment, but they do so at a cost. Supposedly that cost is in our ability to generalize to real world settings. Given that most of us ultimately aspire to explain what goes on in the real world, not just in some laboratory, that cost can be steep indeed. But what if the whole premise that there must be a trade-off between internal and external validity is simply wrong?

In one respect, population-based experiments pose an obvious challenge to that basic tenet. By combining representative population samples with rigorous experimental designs, they demonstrate that internal validity can be had without sacrificing the generalizability of the study's sample of participants. In addition, people need not be extracted from their everyday settings in order to participate in an experiment. These challenges to the orthodoxy are noteworthy.

However, as I will argue, there were good reasons to doubt the veracity of this "truism" regarding the tension between internal and external validity long before the advent of population-based experiments. The tendency to make assertions about the generalizability of research results based solely on either the *setting* in which the study was done (i.e., laboratory versus field) or the representativeness of the *subjects* studied reflects a lack of considered thought on this much broader and ultimately more interesting subject.

Chapter Eight

In this chapter I begin with what is probably the most radical and controversial assertion in the entire book, that the external validity of any given study has little to do with whether it was done in a laboratory or a field setting. Moreover, there is no logical or empirical basis for claiming the superiority of one setting over another for purposes of external validity. On the one hand, this unconventional assertion has been acknowledged before.[1] On the other hand, most social scientists continue to operate and write up their research results as if this observation had not occurred to them.

Internal validity, that is, the strength of causal inference that can be drawn in a given study, is indeed closely tied to methodological choice; if one properly executes an experiment, its internal validity will undoubtedly be stronger than any non-experimental study. But the idea that "recourse to the field, though it gives up much internal validity, buys external validity—simply misunderstands the problem. Field studies do not generalize any more than laboratory experiments do."[2] My central point is not that field studies, surveys, or experiments—or any kind of study for that matter—are more or less generalizable; it is simply that methodology alone provides little to no guidance when judging external validity.

To explain this argument, I begin by describing the origins of the traditional view, which is rooted in ideas about the similarity (or lack thereof) between research settings and real world settings. Interestingly, as demonstrated by the early history of experimental design, the logic of *internal* validity is also about the issue of similarity, in this case similarity between experimental conditions. The idea that this can be achieved through random assignment is probably the single most brilliant methodological advance in the social sciences. I suggest that the same logic regarding similarities and differences as applied to internal validity might be applied to the problem of assessing external validity.

In the final section of the chapter, I evaluate population-based experiments on four key dimensions of generalizability: the settings in which research takes place, the research participants, the outcome measures, and the experimental treatments.[3]

---

[1] For example, see Dipboye and Flanagan (1979); Thye (2007).
[2] Zelditch (2007, p. 105).
[3] Shadish, Cook, and Campbell (2002) further refine their discussion of validity into distinctions among four types, including statistical conclusion validity (i.e., the validity of the statistical inference about the association between the independent and dependent variable) and construct validity (i.e., the extent to which operational measures accurately represent the higher order concepts), in addition to internal and external validity. To keep my discussion simple, I use only the more general distinction between internal and external validity (see Campbell and Stanley, 1963).

The Deductive (and Confused) Basis of
Conventional Wisdom

The term *external validity* is commonly used to refer to the consistency of research results produced in different studies using different samples, settings, measures, and treatments. Like others, I have used the term *generalizability* interchangeably with external validity, again referring to whether results found in one study can be projected onto another situation. However, for simplicity's sake, I discuss contributions of population-based experiments to external validity using the broadest common understanding of what generalizability means.[4]

Those conducting observational studies such as surveys commonly argue that this method maximizes external validity because the setting to which they want to generalize *is* the field and often the population under study is the same population to which they hope to generalize. But observational studies remain weak in their ability to produce causal inferences. Laboratory experiments supposedly maximize internal validity, but lack external validity. Or at least so it seems from superficial examination. Therefore, the conventional wisdom regarding the relationship between internal and external validity is that there is necessarily a trade-off between the two.[5]

However, it is worth remembering that, as reviewed in Chapter 1, the key to causal inference is control over, and manipulation of, the independent variable through random assignment, *not* the location in which the research takes place or the people who participate. Nonetheless, these two factors—the research setting (laboratory versus field) and the research design (carefully manipulated versus passively observed independent variables)—are often confounded. Just because non-experimental studies are limited in their ability to attain internal validity does not mean that experiments therefore must be limited in their ability to attain external validity.

Field experiments provide an obvious and widely recognized exception to this purported tension: to the extent that field experiments make it possible to randomly assign people successfully to experimental treatments, they are considered roughly equal to laboratory experiments in the

---

[4] In other words, can one generalize results from the research setting to real world settings, from research participants to those affected in the real world, from the outcome measures used in the study to real world outcomes of interest, and from reactions to the chosen experimental treatment to treatments as they may occur in the real world.

[5] See, for example, Campbell and Stanley (1963) and Shadish, Cook, and Campbell (2002: 490).

strength of causal inferences that may be drawn. In other words, greater internal validity does not necessarily come at the obvious expense of external validity. In cases where the treatments cannot be assured of reaching the correct subjects successfully, field experiments sometimes devolve into quasi-experimental designs, but when they are executed as intended, they are true experiments by virtue of using random assignment to conditions.

But because field experiments are, by definition, executed in more naturalistic settings, it is often erroneously claimed that they, therefore, must have greater external validity than laboratory studies. Results of field experiments are routinely claimed to be more generalizable simply because they are field experiments.

The logic behind this claim is based solely on the similarity of settings. As the conventional wisdom has it, "To generalize you need similarity between the laboratory and real life—that is, field settings; lab and field settings are very dissimilar; therefore generalization is not justified (or highly dubious)."[6] On the one hand, experiments do seem inherently contrived and artificial when compared to field studies (whether experimental or observational). On the other hand, why should we be so quick to assume that results from one particular field setting will easily generalize to another, completely different, real world setting?

Upon further examination, there is nothing particularly logical about such a claim. To borrow an example from a famous survey in my own field of study, why should the way people in Erie County, Ohio, decide for whom to vote for President necessarily tell us more about how the country as a whole decides than an experimental study relying on a convenience sample? For the most part, field studies use convenience samples, although they are typically somewhat larger in size than those used in lab studies. But why should we necessarily believe that a small, highly politically stable Midwestern town produces more generalizable results than a laboratory study executed with a small, but perhaps more politically diverse sample of participants? Field studies have their own problems with generalization; as one experimental economist pointed out, field studies of sumo wrestlers, sports-card traders, or coin collectors "cannot be seamlessly extrapolated to other economic settings."[7]

The logic behind this assumption is that there is always greater "realism" in the field than in the lab and greater similarity between the so-called real world and the field. Unfortunately, this deductive reasoning is problematic because next to nothing is known about the bases for generalizability.[8] As Cook and Campbell pointed out, external validity is necessarily an induc-

[6] Locke (1986, p. 3).
[7] Levitt and List (2007, p. 170).
[8] Locke (1986).

tive process, not a deductive one.[9] For example, one cannot deductively infer from the fact that a study is a field experiment that its findings are therefore more externally valid.[10] Instead, it is only from an accumulation of studies or results across different settings and subpopulations, that one can increase the inductive probability that generalization holds under various circumstances. The variation among laboratory studies and among field studies is as great as the variation between lab and field studies. As a result, discussing the issue deductively amounts to "idle speculation."[11] Any given field setting is no more inherently generalizable than any given laboratory setting.

Thus far I have argued against a common, but simplistic assumption about the trade-off between internal and external validity. Further, I have suggested that using the setting in which a study was executed or the type of research design as a guide to its overall generalizability is unwarranted. Generic claims about the extent of generalizability of a study's results simply because it was done in the field or in the lab are misleading.

To be clear, my more general point is not that field studies or laboratory experiments are or are not more generalizable, but rather that social scientists have chosen an inaccurate, inappropriate heuristic on which to base these conclusions. Because a study is done in a lab is not a legitimate reason to question its generalizability any more than the fact that a study is done in the field automatically confers generalizability.

So what is a researcher to do to assess external validity? If one cannot make a deductive claim based on the type of study that was done, what can one say? The best approach is, not surprisingly, the least practical. Rather than asserting generalizability solely based on a research setting, generalizability should be a focus for empirical inquiry. Ideally, scholars should investigate this question empirically by comparing results from studies in one setting (or using one particular population or treatment) with another. The way to approach this issue would be to ask whether the findings related to a given hypothesis are consistent across settings, subjects, and so forth. In other words, researchers need to pay greater attention to homogeneity and heterogeneity of effects.

This practice has been done to a very limited extent in some areas of research through meta-analysis. For example, in the late 1970s, a review of the literature in industrial and organizational psychology suggested that field research was just as narrow as experimental studies in the actors, behaviors, and settings that were studied. Experiments relied heavily

[9] Cook and Campbell (1976, p. 236).
[10] See Green and Gerber (2003) for an example of the common kind of deductive conclusion about external validity based on research design.
[11] Fromkin and Streufert (1976, p. 457).

on college students, but field studies relied just as heavily on samples of certain kinds of employees in certain kinds of organizations in one type of industry.[12]

A slightly different approach was used to address whether aggression as measured in laboratory settings generalized beyond the lab. By looking at whether correlates of aggression in real world situations (both individual differences and situational variables) were also correlates in the lab setting, Anderson and Bushman drew largely positive conclusions about the generalizability of laboratory studies of aggression.[13] Although not designed explicitly toward this end, a recent meta-analysis of the intergroup contact effect in social psychology illuminated differences in the impact of intergroup contact across different settings, and thus shed light on what it is about the setting that matters and what does not.[14]

But in the absence of available meta-analyses (as is most often the case), or the time to do one's own, how can scholars assess the generalizability of findings from any individual study? What should be the basis for such claims? Ultimately I suggest that study design alone should be supplanted with a consideration of the similarities between the research setting, participants, treatments, and outcomes in the study itself relative to the contexts in which the theory is argued to apply. Unfortunately, similarities in settings and participants have dominated the discussion to date. But even if we agree on these general standards, "similiarity" is itself a slippery term.

To better understand the role of similarity in assessing external validity, I turn to a parallel problem that emerges in assessing internal validity. Although my discussion of internal validity may seem a bit tangential at first, both concepts force scholars to grapple with the issue of similarity and difference, particularly the question of how similar is similar enough to make the claims we wish to make.

THE INTERNAL VALIDITY PARALLEL: HOW SIMILAR IS SIMILAR ENOUGH?

As reviewed in Chapter 1, the historical development of experimental methods centers on the issue of how to deal with the problem of "third variables" or spurious causes in inferring causation. Experiments address the problem of spuriousness through random assignment of subjects to

[12] Dipboye and Flanagan (1979).
[13] Anderson and Bushman (1997).
[14] Pettigrew and Tropp (2006).

conditions. Although this approach seems intuitively logical to those who encounter it today, it is worth noting that this was not always the case.

Experimentation as a solution to the problem of third variables emanated directly from John Stuart Mill's "method of difference":

> If an instance in which the phenomenon under investigation occurs, and an instance in which it does not occur, have every circumstance in common save one, that one occurring only in the former, the circumstance in which alone the two instances differ is the effect, or cause, or an indispensable part of the cause, of the phenomenon.[15]

Unfortunately, there is no practical way to achieve Mill's difference criterion—that is, to have "every circumstance in common save one." In the real world, no two circumstances are exactly alike, and any two empirical instances differ in more than one way, opening the door for other potential causes. So while the logic behind the method of difference is appealing, it lacks practicality.

Probability theory provides a solution to this problem. By means of random assignment, Ronald Fisher argued, we can make two circumstances similar to one another save for one difference.[16] Random assignment equates at the group, rather than the individual, level. And conveniently, it equates groups not only on factors the researcher has thought of, but also on those she has not thought of, as well as many factors that are completely irrelevant. Thus we assume that if the differences in the dependent variable that we observe between experimental groups after treatment are unlikely to have occurred by chance, then they are empirical regularities that are worthy of note.

As revised by Fisher's probabilistic approach, Mill's method of difference is the underlying theoretical basis for most contemporary experimentation in the social sciences. Nonetheless, this solution has not gone without criticism and misunderstanding. Is random assignment really the cure-all it seems? Some have raised concerns because random assignment only truly "equates" experimental groups with infinite sample sizes.[17] Since most experiments utilize relatively small samples, and come nowhere near this standard, is it not possible that there is some unknown causal factor (i.e., a third variable) that accounts for the observed relationship and thus threatens the validity of a causal interpretation? Particularly if there are large numbers of potential spurious causes for an observed

---

[15] From Mill (1843, p. 455).
[16] See Fischer (1935, 1956).
[17] Cohen (1989, 1997).

relationship, the chance that the experimental groups will differ on at least one of these potentially spurious variables seems quite high: "As the number of unknown or unknowable 3rd (spurious) causes increases, the probability that an experimental and control group will differ on at least one of these variables approaches 1.0."[18]

When done correctly, randomization should produce groups that are highly similar to one another. But even when executed perfectly, randomization is unlikely to equate groups on an infinite number of potential comparisons. In fact, chance alone tells us that in around 5 comparisons out of 100, experimental and control groups will differ significantly on some variable. While it is true that no one does experiments with sample sizes approaching infinity, and thus expects identical experimental conditions, it is not therefore true that experimental results are highly susceptible to mistaken inferences.

But why not, given the typically small experimental sample sizes? The beauty of random assignment is not that it guarantees equivalence between experimental and control groups on all possible variables, but rather that the expected sum of any differences between groups across all variables is zero. Thus, excessive handwringing about perfect similarity across groups is unwarranted because the variables on which the groups may, in fact, differ are highly likely to be normally distributed with a mean of zero. In other words, the effects of these known and unknown variables on the dependent variable should largely cancel one another out, with no net effect to undermine interpretation of the effects of the experimental manipulation.

Although experiments are widely regarded as the best possible design for establishing internal validity because of their ability to rule out potentially spurious relationships as well as reverse causation, this elevated status *does not require* perfect similarity across experimental conditions. The experimental groups need not be identical to one another in order for the logic of internal validity to hold. As discussed in the next section, this same issue of degrees of similarity emerges in the context of external validity as well.

EXTERNAL VALIDITY: HOW SIMILAR IS SIMILAR ENOUGH?

How similar must a study be to another situation in order to justify a claim that the results will generalize? Perhaps more importantly, in what respects should the research setting, subjects, treatment, and outcomes be similar to the situation to which it is being generalized? To date, almost nothing is

---

[18] Cohen (1997, p. 74).

known about the legitimate basis for generalization,[19] and there is no one accepted definition of generalizability either.[20]

As with internal validity, similarity (or the lack thereof) has been the basis for longstanding assumptions about the lack of generalizability of results from laboratory experiments. With external validity, it is the level of similarity between the "real world" and the research setting that is most often held to be key. Field settings are argued to be more similar to the real world than are experimental settings; therefore, field settings are assumed to be more generalizable. Or at least so the argument goes.

Much has been made of the artificiality of laboratory environments and how different they are from the real world. As Ilgen notes, "Laboratory experiments by their very nature cannot create designs that truly represent all, or even most, of the conditions present in naturally occurring settings populated by people who exist, interact and behave in these settings over a long period."[21] How similar does a research setting need to be to the external setting to which one would like to generalize in order to support an assertion about external validity? And what about the similarity of research participants, treatments, and outcomes? With external validity we thus face the same question once again: How similar is similar enough? Scholars tend to assume that unless the actors, context, and activity in the lab are exactly the same as in the real world, then generalization is automatically suspect.

This kind of knee-jerk reaction is unwarranted. Clearly they need not be identical, or else generalizability would be a non-issue; if it were only legitimate to generalize to other instances in the exact same setting, with the exact same subjects in which the research itself was done, then generalization itself would be irrelevant, as would most of our research findings. Exact replications tell us nothing about the generalizability of results.

In discussions of internal validity, scholars have used the terms *essential* and *incidental* similarity to identify the dimensions that are relevant and irrelevant to similarity across experimental conditions, respectively. These same terms can be applied to similarities between research settings and their targets of generalization. Some similarities and differences are incidental, while others are essential for generalization.

So what types of essential differences should affect the generalization of findings? Again, there is no way to determine this deductively. Some subfields of research that have examined this issue empirically may provide guidance. They suggest that "a detailed point-by-point similarity with

---

[19] Many scholars have made this point over the years, including Cook and Campbell (1976), Locke et al. (1986), and others, but the argument has largely fallen on deaf ears.
[20] Cook and Campbell (1976) outline at least four different possibilities.
[21] Ilgen (1986, p. 257).

respect to subjects, tasks, settings and so forth is not necessarily required in order to achieve generalizability."[22]

So far, so good. The problem may not be as intractable as it first seems. But we still have no easy way to figure out what is essential and what is incidental. At the moment, researchers are free to seize on any dimension of similarity to argue for generalizability. One of my favorite such examples involves potato chips. In laboratory studies of political advertising, for example, it is often mentioned that subjects sat on a couch and ate potato chips while they were viewing the television program. It is true that many of us eat junk food while watching television, myself included. But implicit in taking up valuable journal space in order to tell readers about the chips is the assumption that by making the laboratory setting more like the real world context for television viewing, the researchers have increased the generalizability of their laboratory findings. Should this convince readers that results from this laboratory are more generalizable as a result?

Maybe. But I remain skeptical about just how essential potato chips are to the process of political persuasion and attitude change; maybe even the couch is irrelevant.[23] The sheer fact that they are mentioned is testimony to our lack of a sensible basis for establishing generalizability. What is ultimately required in order to sort out essential versus incidental similarity is far more than a cursory consideration of snack food. For any given hypothesis, it requires a thoughtful consideration of setting, subjects, outcome measures, and treatments.

THE GENERALIZABILITY OF POPULATION-BASED EXPERIMENTS

Absent a pre-existing meta-analysis outlining conditions under which an empirical regularity appears, what is appropriate to claim? How much should you just "give in" to the common heuristic that experiments probably lack generalizability simply because they are experiments?

Little, if at all. To repeat, there is no deductive or empirical basis for claiming that experimental findings are less generalizable than those of other methods. Just because experiments are high on internal validity does not make them low on external validity. Moreover, when it comes to population-based survey experiments, researchers are on much firmer ground than usual in many respects.

[22] Locke (1986, p. 6).
[23] To put all of my own cards on the table, I will admit that I also used to have a couch in my lab, but I remain unconvinced that it contributed to the external validity of my findings.

Some social scientists have pointed out that true external validity is only possible from the convergence of many different studies,[24] a point that is well taken. When such accumulations exist, then this is obviously the best route to evaluating generalizability. However, in practice, most of us are asked to comment on the generalizability of findings from individual studies based on analytic logic alone. So making such judgments is probably unavoidable, even if they are at best educated guesses.

Researchers should take into account four major considerations in evaluating the likely degree of generalizability of a population-based experiment: setting, participants, measures, and treatments. In considering how much each of these four dimensions is similar to the "real world," two forms of realism are worth considering. "Experimental realism" refers to whether what happens in the experiment appears real to the subject, whereas "mundane realism" refers to whether the experimental situation resembles situations encountered in the real world. Intuitively one might expect these two kinds of realism to be highly positively correlated, but this is not necessarily the case.

For example, when Solomon Asch famously demonstrated that judgments about the length of a line could be influenced by the judgments of others, he also demonstrated that mundane and experimental realism could be entirely different within a given study. As Asch varied the number of confederates who gave wrong answers about the actual length of a line, he likewise altered the percentage of subjects who conformed and reported similarly inaccurate judgments.[25] On one hand, the Asch setting had tremendous experimental realism, as evidenced by the extreme discomfort many subjects felt when asked to judge the length of the lines. They truly believed that the line length judgments of other participants were for some reason very different from their own. At the same time, the experiment had incredibly low levels of mundane realism because it is next to impossible to find such a strange situation occurring in the real world, that is, one in which one's own visual perceptions are so at odds with others'. Asch induced unusually high levels of conformity in his lab by creating a situation in which there was no other explanation that people could come up with for the difference between their view and others' perceptions. By contrast, in most of the real world situations to which people want to generalize Asch's results, there is, indeed, some alternative explanation for differing views.[26] Do devout anti-abortion Catholics rack their

---

[24] For example, Liyanarachchi (2007).
[25] Asch (1952).
[26] See Ross, Bierbrauer, and Hoffman (1976).

brains for an explanation of their difference of opinion from pro-choice feminists? I seriously doubt it.[27]

Mundane realism tends to be derogated by advocates of experimental methods as less important than experimental realism, perhaps because it is far easier to produce experimental realism in the lab than it is mundane realism. And besides, mundane realism is so . . . mundane. But as the example above demonstrates, both are arguably equally important if we really care about generalizing findings to the real world. Without experimental realism, internal validity becomes suspect. Subjects must "buy in" to the experimental situation so that the treatments work to bring about the intended change in the independent variable, or else the experiment simply stops in its tracks. Manipulation checks can usually be included to ensure that treatments have worked as intended in influencing the independent variable, but there is no "check" for mundane realism. External validity thus remains subject to judgment.

Next I address each of the four dimensions on which this judgment should be rendered, with particular attention to how population-based experiments fare relative to field experiments (generally thought to have high generalizability) and relative to laboratory experiments (generally thought to have low generalizability).

Setting

For whatever reason, similarities between research settings and real world settings tend to be emphasized to a much greater degree than the other three factors, rivaled only secondarily by concerns over the generalizability of subjects. There is no evidence, to my knowledge, that settings *should* weigh more heavily in generalizability than any of these other factors. Do population-based experiments generally have acceptable levels of both experimental and mundane realism with respect to their settings? Although assessments must ultimately be made on a study by study basis, relative to laboratory experiments, the setting for population-based experiments usually has more mundane realism. People serve as participants answering questions from their homes or offices, where there is little likelihood of arousing suspicion about experimental treatments, or even awareness that one is taking part in an experiment. People know they are taking part in a study that involves answering questions, to be sure, but guarded and suspicious reactions are far more likely when a participant enters a laboratory on a university campus. In addition, pro-social behavior tends to be ac-

---

[27] For a discussion of the limited generalizability of conformity findings see Ross, Bierbrauer, and Hoffman (1976). For their application to political attitudes in particular, see Mutz (1998).

centuated in the lab, where people are under close supervision, a concern that should lessen in a population-based experiment where no human is directly observing.[28] Both being in a laboratory and being observed by others may detract from the extent to which laboratory behaviors are generalizable relative to behavior in population-based experiments.

Indeed, the natural variation in settings provided by population-based experiments is, by most standards, preferable to a traditional experimental environment, even if it is not directly manipulable. Nothing says experiment more loudly and clearly than stepping into a "laboratory." And even if there is no nameplate as such on the door, most lay people associate taking part in a university study with participating in an experiment. When they take part in a survey from the privacy of their own home or office, the same baggage is likely missing. And thanks to the visual and audio capabilities provided by Internet connections, it is now possible to administer complex multi-media treatments without stepping into a laboratory.

Experimental realism may be more problematic for population-based experiments. Contextual factors cannot be controlled as carefully by the researcher, and this may introduce noise that makes it more difficult to successfully execute experimental treatments and detect underlying effects. On the other hand, while there is a common assumption that the high level of control found in a laboratory is necessary in order to create experimental realism, the connection between control and realism is not obvious.[29] To get people to react to the treatment in a population-based experiment, the consequences of their participation must be made to seem as real as possible. As discussed in the preceding chapters, in many cases such consequences can indeed be "real," as when one donates money to a cause as part of an experimental study.

Based on the studies described in this book, I am dubious that experimental realism is a severe limitation of population-based experiments relative to lab studies. As evidenced in Part I, many successful experimental manipulations have been accomplished via the content of population-based treatments, even manipulations of concepts largely thought to be culturally determined or stabilized by early adulthood.[30] Experimental realism is usually greater in the context of a field experiment, but researchers often lack the ability to ensure that the treatments have actually reached subjects, an issue that is far less problematic in population-based experiments. If the manipulation check suggests that one has effectively brought about the desired change in the independent variable, the most difficult hurdle has already been overcome. If the level of experimental realism is

---

[28] Benz and Meier (2008).
[29] Berkowitz and Donnerstein (1982).
[30] See, for example, the studies of social trust described in Chapter 6.

high enough in a given setting for the experimental treatment to produce a significant manipulation check, demonstrating that the treatment brought about the desired change in the independent variable, then it is probably also adequate for producing the outcome of interest in the dependent variable. Both require experimental realism; the main problem is that many researchers neglect to include manipulation checks in their designs.

If desired, social context and other forms of variation in settings can be explicitly incorporated into the design and analysis of population-based experiments. For example, many researchers suggest that social context often conditions treatment effects,[31] which seems a definite possibility for many social science theories. For example, if there is social support for a given kind of behavior in the environment, it may be far easier to induce than when there is not. When the relevant characteristic of settings cannot be manipulated as part of the design, the solution is to measure and block on the relevant characteristics of social context in order to understand the extent to which they matter and thus improve the efficiency of the design.

The more serious limitations on the generalizability of settings involve restrictions on the time frame.[32] Of course, all studies must be done in a particular time and place, so this is not unique to experiments. But both laboratory and population-based experiments tend to be short-term, one-time interventions with one-time measures of the outcome of interest. This problem is not inherent in the method, but it is a common restriction due to limited research budgets. It is always more time-consuming and costly to track subjects down later and/or induce them to return to the lab for a second or third time. But it can be done. Moreover, as discussed in Chapter 6, the structure of ongoing Internet panels makes re-contact easier and less expensive, and thus entirely plausible in the context of population-based survey experiments.

Participants

Population-based survey experiments have obvious advantages in terms of the generalizability of the sample population. This is the dimension on which population-based survey experiments win the external validity contest hands-down. The diversity of samples available through surveys means that population-based experiments can address generalizability across different segments of the population, far beyond college sophomores, to many educational and economic groups within the population.

But the advantages do not end with generalizability to the full population of interest. The subjects in a population-based experiment can be repre-

[31] See for example, Gaines and Kuklinski (2010).
[32] See Levitt and List (2007) for a full discussion.

sentative of just about any group to which the researcher desires to generalize. They can easily transcend local geography, and allow us to test theories on precisely those groups to which we expect the theories to generalize.

Does this matter? Opinions differ, but it certainly does not hurt. Sometimes, as in the studies of jealousy described in Chapter 3, there are logical reasons to question the generalizability of findings from student samples in particular; in other cases, it is unclear whether it should matter or not. Whether findings will be different is likely to vary by the topic and process under study. My own view is that there are very few areas of social science in which we can safely assume (without any empirical evidence) that findings based on students are generalizable to other populations. There are some, to be sure. But there are far more examples in which it was prematurely assumed that a finding based on college students was a good approximation of what would be found outside the student context. In a study of consumer behavior, for example, non-college student subjects generated effect sizes that were, on average, 42 percent higher than college student samples.[33] Others have experienced failures to replicate across student and non-student populations.[34] In economic experiments using the dictator game, for example, community members donated significantly more money on average than students.[35]

Although field experiments are commonly lauded for their high level of generalizability on the dimensions of settings and subjects, they are seldom as diverse on either dimension as one might obtain from a population-based experiment. Because field experiments usually require the cooperation of public officials, they are often limited to a local geographic area where the practical limitations of experimenting on the general public can more easily be surmounted. For example, even an extensive series of field experiments on voter turnout that went to great lengths to demonstrate external validity still had important limitations on its samples. Participants were limited to those in a particular city or state, those on heavily residential streets, or to cities and towns where radio advertisements were particularly affordable.[36] For obvious reasons, practical matters tend to constrain field experimental samples. When chosen with a theory in mind, population-based experiments can render concerns about the generalizability of participants completely moot.

Often the larger problem for researchers is deciding what the appropriate target population should be for a given study. Say, for example, that

---

[33] Peterson, Albaum, and Beltramini (1985).

[34] For example, Mintz, Redd, and Vedlitz (2006).

[35] Carpenter, Connolly, and Myers (2008).

[36] Gerber and Green (2000a, 2000b, 2001); Gerber, Green, and Larimer (2008); Gerber, Green, and Shachar (2003); Green and Gerber (2004); Krasno and Green (2008); Panagopoulos and Green (2008).

one wants to assess the extent of learning from political talk shows. One could do a population-based experiment exposing a random sample of the population to a representative program, and then evaluate learning. However, skeptics might claim that learning effects would be overestimated in such a study because few of the politically uninterested people in the sample would ever actually watch such a program in real life. So what is the alternative? One possibility is to filter out those who never watch such programs before randomly assigning people to conditions. Another possibility is to begin by asking respondents whether they watch any of a variety of specific talk shows, and then block on watchers and non-watchers as they occur in the real world. In this fashion, the size of the treatment effect could be known for both those who generally watch such programs and those who generally do not.[37] Most importantly, to choose an appropriate target population to sample in such a study, it is essential to decide whether the research question is how much political talk shows could potentially educate the general public, or how much they already do so in the real world, given those who choose to watch them.

Measurement of Outcomes

Scholars typically think in terms of settings and participants when assessing external validity, but standardized approaches to measurement of the dependent variable probably create far more generalizability problems. This is easily the most underexplored dimension of generalizability, and roughly equally so across surveys, experiments, and field studies. Do findings generalize across different operationalizations of the same concept? Once a given operationalization "works" in a survey or experimental context, there is a tendency to replicate using the exact same operationalization over and over. But if findings turn out to be dependent upon a specific operationalization of the concept, this limitation provides important new pieces of information about the external validity of the study.

Where do population-based experiments fall in their relative neglect of this dimension of generalizability? When it comes to the *ability* to generalize beyond specific operationalizations, population-based experiments certainly have the capacity to do so, even within a single experiment. But in practice this is done less often than it should be, perhaps because of length/money restrictions, but also out of habit. One good example of a population-based experiment addressing the generalizability of dependent measures is the fidelity study described in Chapter 3. In addition to assessing whether the standard finding (men value sexual fidelity whereas

[37] Gaines and Kuklinski (2008) suggest a somewhat different approach to the same general problem, attempting to simulate self-selection in the context of the experiment itself.

women care more about emotional fidelity) would replicate on a sample that has more relationship and life experience than college sophomores, the authors also simultaneously examined the generalizability of the key dependent measure used in this research paradigm.[38]

The widely replicated operationalization of the dependent measure used in this research, first developed by Buss and his colleagues, is a forced-choice question about whether emotional or sexual infidelity would be more upsetting or distressing:

> Please think of a serious or committed relationship that you have had in the past, that you currently have, or that you would like to have. Imagine that you discover that the person with whom you've been seriously involved became interested in someone else. What would upset or distress you more?
>
> - Imagining your partner falling in love and forming a deep emotional attachment to that person.
> - Imagining your partner having sexual intercourse with that person.[39]

Some argued that the usual finding was an artifact of the single forced-choice item used in this line of research, and advocated instead asking which type of infidelity would make the respondent more angry, more hurt, and more likely to blame their partner.[40] Results suggested that there was merit to these concerns. The original finding was not generalizable across alternative measures and samples, a discovery that ultimately deepened psychologists' understanding of this well-known pattern.

The whole point of doing a population-based experiment rather than a laboratory experiment is to improve external validity. Nonetheless, researchers seldom consider the generalizability of their dependent measures, even when executing population-based experiments. To take full advantage of this technique, researchers should make use of the unusually large sample sizes by trying more than one operationalization of the central outcome.

Although I hesitate to speak for any entire field of study, I have the strong impression that fields emphasizing external validity, such as political science, generally tend to give measurement issues short shrift. Because of the heavy reliance on surveys, and the high cost per survey question, there is a tendency to rely on single item indicators, even for the all-important

---

[38] Green and Sabini (2006).
[39] Buss et al. (1992); Buss (2000).
[40] Green and Sabini (2006).

dependent variable. Surveys generally try to capture a large number of variables during one extensive interview, and the data are collected to test dozens of different hypotheses.

Fields that emphasize laboratory work and student samples tend to use more multi-item measures and indexes, perhaps because once a subject is in the lab, there is seldom much additional cost per question asked, so it makes sense to ask more questions rather than fewer. Thus the driving forces behind measurement decisions tend to be different inside and outside of the lab. Whereas experiments will go into greater depth in measuring concepts related to one particular topic, surveys are more often omnibus instruments. The pattern I describe need not necessarily be the case, but I think it is a fairly accurate caricature of standard practice.

Moreover, because many large-scale surveys such as the General Social Survey and the American National Election Study are institutionalized for purposes of studying longitudinal trends, these indicators seldom change from year to year, thus providing little evidence of generalizability of findings across different operationalizations of the same concept. In field experiments, the constraints of the setting may make crude measures of the outcome the best that is attainable.

In my experience with TESS investigators from different fields, I noted that internal validity-oriented researchers (such as psychologists) would argue that they could not possibly measure a given concept without a 20-item battery, whereas external validity-oriented researchers (such as political scientists) would use that same allocation of 20 items to measure 20 different concepts, one item each. For some fields of study, the desire to measure many different constructs is a force of habit that stems from a fear of missing that key third variable or spurious influence, the control variable that would allow for the strongest possible causal argument. One can never have too many control variables!

But when running a population-based experiment, such an approach makes little sense. The spuriousness problem has already been taken care of by the design itself, so there is no need to measure 20 different concepts. Ideally, investigators would use whatever additional time/space they have on a survey to implement alternative measures of the dependent variable instead. In this way, population-based experiments could serve to increase knowledge of whether results generalize across different kinds of measures.

Another approach to generalization of measurement that makes population-based experiments especially useful is when researchers gather both attitudinal and behavioral measures such as intent to donate and actual donating behavior. For example, in a study of determinants of generosity toward Katrina victims, Fong and Luttmer found that the amounts suggested in response to a hypothetical giving question were far lower than the actual amount that respondents gave.[41] According to one analysis, the use of a behavioral response measure in consumer studies resulted in an 85 percent increase in effect size relative to one based on self-report.[42]

In general, I would not go so far as to claim that the population-based experiment—nor any other method for that matter—has an inherent advantage with respect to the generalization of outcome measures. But given that there is no need to measure huge numbers of third variables (relative to a survey), thus allowing for the inclusion of a wide variety of both attitudinal and behavioral outcome measures, population-based experiments certainly *can* be profitably used for this purpose. Moreover, the larger sample size characterizing population-based experiments means that there is often enough statistical power to essentially run an experiment within an experiment, randomly assigning subjects to different operationalizations of the dependent variable to see if results vary. These additional experimental factors can be added into the design and analysis just like any other independent variable, thus allowing assessment of the robustness of treatment effects using different outcome measures across conditions. Questionable self-report measures of attitudes and behaviors can be verified either by actual behavioral measures (e.g., donating money) or by later self-reports on real behaviors.

It is unfortunate that few researchers to date have taken advantage of these opportunities when implementing population-based experiments, especially because this approach makes it easier than other methods. The reason they have not been used toward this end thus far is because population-based experiments are still in a bit of a honeymoon period at the moment. Most scholars are happy enough to be able to generalize treatment effects to non-student samples and have therefore not yet delved into other dimensions of generalizability.

Treatments

Whether an experimental treatment is generalizable or not refers to whether *another* manipulation of the same independent variable would produce the same experimental effect. If it does not, and the effect depends on something that is unique to that particular treatment, then it casts doubt on the veracity of the abstract theory.

Some criticisms of population-based experimental treatments suggest that they are necessarily less "natural" than what might happen in the real

---

[41] Fong and Luttmer (2009). See also Alpizar, Carlsson, and Johansson-Stenman (2008) for an example drawn from economics.
[42] Peterson, Albaum, and Beltramini (1985).

world; in other words, criticism focuses on the mundane realism of the stimulus. If true, the implications of these differences are unclear. Some suggest that findings from population-based experimental treatments will underestimate real world effect sizes because treatments are often fleeting, one-shot exposures, whereas the real world includes repeated exposure. Others suggest that population-based treatment effects will be unreasonably large for many of the same reasons that effects tend to be larger in the lab than in the field; levels of attention may be unusually high relative to real world contexts, or the relevant population may not be the one that was sampled.

Scholars need to be careful to differentiate concerns about the similarity of the treatment to what happens in the real world that causes the *independent variable* to change, and the generalizability of that treatment's *effects*. Take, for example, the study of the effects of social trust on purchasing behavior described in Chapter 6. Social trust was influenced using a tailored treatment centered on a *Reader's Digest* article. This turned out to be an effective way to manipulate social trust, but no one is arguing that when social trust declines it is typically because too many people are reading *Reader's Digest*. The important thing is that social trust was effectively manipulated, as demonstrated by a manipulation check.

If another completely different stimulus designed to lower social trust also successfully affected levels of social trust, but in this case without influencing purchasing behavior (the central dependent variable), then one would have reason to suspect that there was something unique about the *Reader's Digest* treatment. Perhaps something more than just social trust was driving the effect. Why should the results of one treatment to lower social trust not generalize to another treatment that also lowered social trust? In short, the purpose of the study is to see whether change in the independent variable (by whatever means) produces change in the dependent variable, not to simulate the sources of change in social trust.

Unfortunately, seldom are those making claims about the lack of generalizability in various studies comparing apples to apples. For example, in one recent study that compared survey results from before and after new information was released in the news to population-based experimental results providing all respondents with similar information, the authors argue that population-based experiments overestimate real world effects because there is stronger evidence of learning in response to the experimental treatments than in the cross-sectional surveys bracketing the news release.[43] They conclude that population-based experiments "at least on this topic, generate effects that are only observed among parts of the pop-

[43] Barabas and Jerit (2010).

ulation who are likely to be exposed to treatment messages or predisposed to accept them."[44]

Upon reflection, however, this very statement points to the problematic nature of the comparison. The observational study does not assure exposure to the experimental treatment; those who are not exposed to the information of interest obviously cannot learn it. Thus while the population-based experiment generates an estimate of *learning given exposure*, the observational study estimates average learning among some who have *and* some who have not been exposed to the message. By comparing experimental effect sizes to those respondents in the survey who have higher levels of media exposure, the comparison is made somewhat more comparable, but it is not surprising to find weaker effects in the latter group. A population-based experiment (or any experiment, for that matter) cannot tell us how many people are likely to be exposed to a given treatment in the real world. But this is not the same problem as a lack of generalizability; the ideal "apples to apples" comparison of effects would be between those who were exposed to the same message within the two different designs.

This same misunderstanding is evident when scholars complain that framing experiments "typically obliterate the distinction between the supply of information, on the one hand, and its consumption, on the other. That is, experiments are normally carried out in such a way that virtually everyone receives the message. . . . By ensuring that frames reach their intended audiences, experiments may exaggerate their power."[45] Experiments estimate effects given exposure; nothing more and nothing less. If one wanted to examine whether or not people encounter frames, rather than whether they will be affected by them if exposed, then a survey would be far better suited to that research question.[46] By combining knowledge of the extent of exposure to the message with evidence of the extent of impact given reception, one could conceivably estimate its real world impact. In some circumstances population-based experiments can *combine* both of these functions in a single study, thus making them even more advantageous relative to either surveys or experiments alone.

But differences in exposure are not the only basis for concern about "unrealistically powerful" manipulations in experimental designs.[47] Similar

---

[44] Barabas and Jerit (2008, p. 1).

[45] Kinder (2007, p. 157).

[46] A lack of control over the timing of exposure to the treatment in the field makes exact comparisons even more problematic. In population-based experiments, the researcher knows precisely when the subject is exposed to the treatment and for how long. In the field, by contrast even among those who are exposed, it is difficult to know who was exposed to what when, and thus short-term recall and long-term recall may be confounded.

[47] Kinder and Palfrey (1993, p. 27).

issues have been raised by those pointing out that many treatments—such as experimental demonstrations of framing effects—are unrealistic because these effects are regularly cancelled out in the real world by competing frames.[48] The argument here is not that the frames are effective in population-based experiments while ineffective in the real world, but rather that the field includes more than just one isolated framing stimulus. This would seem self-evidently true. But one cannot logically claim that A is *not* an influence on Y simply because B *also* influences Y in the opposite direction. In the real world as well as in the lab, the people exposed to any given influence bring with them the impact of myriad other influences, some canceling and some reinforcing. The important point is that due to random assignment, those extraneous influences should net to zero. The whole point of an experiment is to isolate the effects of treatment, so this is a strength rather than a weakness of population-based survey experiments.

These misunderstandings of the purpose of some experiments are less consequential than two other problems with generalizability that could, indeed, lead to overestimation of real world effects. One possibility is that even if the same kind of people are exposed to a given piece of information or treatment in the real world as well, the distraction of other stories or activities means that they process it in a fundamentally different way in a population-based experiment and thus are never affected by it. Unlike the preceding examples, this is a genuine external validity problem. In both cases participants are exposed to the treatment, but in one setting they are not influenced by it due to distraction.

A second circumstance under which generalizability issues arise is when the estimate of impact is based on one subset of the population that experiences forced exposure in an experimental setting, but in the real world the susceptible group would never encounter the treatment. Based on the initial definition of population-based experiments that I offered, this technically should not happen. Recall that in Chapter 1, population-based survey experiments are defined as experiments in which the participants are purposely representative of the target population of interest for a given theory. It is worth keeping in mind that representative national samples are not always the ideal population, for this very reason. For example, given that those who are uninterested in politics do not pay much attention to political programming, the fact that they *could be* persuaded, if exposed, may be somewhat irrelevant to understanding political persuasion as a naturally-occurring, real world phenomena.[49]

The correct population to sample will depend upon one's research purpose. If a researcher's goal were to estimate an average treatment effect

---

[48] Sniderman and Theriault (2004).
[49] See Zaller (1992) for a full explanation.

for all who could potentially be exposed, then a national sample might be appropriate. On the other hand, if the researcher's goal were to estimate the size of effects specifically among those who are likely to be exposed to a message, then the population of interest might be limited to the politically interested and involved.

If the correct target population is unknown, population-based experiments can be especially advantageous relative to lab experiments because the diversity of the sample helps researchers determine who is more susceptible within a population. If it is feasible to include pre-test survey questions to provide some purchase on who is most likely to be exposed to a given treatment in the real world, then the researcher can essentially have her cake and eat it too. If one knows both who is likely to be exposed to the treatment in the real world, *and* the size of the effect on that subpopulation, this knowledge will go a long way toward accurately estimating effect size in the real world.

THE ROLE OF SIMILARITY

To summarize, the role of similarity is central to a complete understanding of the advantages and disadvantages of various empirical methods, but the nature of its importance is widely misunderstood. With respect to internal validity, anything short of perfect similarity across experimental conditions is often perceived as a threat to internal validity, when this is far from the case. Likewise, with respect to external validity, researchers often seek to maximize similarities between the real world in which the effect is believed to occur, and the research setting. But generalizability is about many factors beyond setting alone. Population-based survey experiments are especially helpful in increasing external validity via the diversity of experimental participants, but they can also be used to examine generalizability through variations in treatments and outcome measures.

Moreover, the real world is a highly heterogeneous place. Unlike the inherent advantages in establishing internal validity that come with random assignment, the path to better external validity is not through using any particular methodical approach. Seeking greater diversity in subjects, implementation of experimental treatments, settings, and outcome measures is the best way to establish external validity.

Population-based survey experiments are beneficial because they combine the internal validity of experimental designs with tremendous advantages in external validity. An experimental design does indeed guarantee an important degree of internal validity. The internal validity of randomized experiments is already without peer. Thus population-based experiments have an automatic leg up on observational and quasi-experimental designs because they are true experiments. Moreover, this approach often retains greater control over random assignment and exposure to treatments than field experiments are able to accomplish.[50] All of the standard requirements for inferring causality are easily met by design.

Population-based experiments also have at least one additional advantage bearing on their ability to detect effects. Their large samples sizes make it easier to detect effects that are difficult to find amidst the fog of individual differences. Even relatively subtle effects may be identified fairly readily, at least more readily than in a laboratory study with equally diverse subjects but a much smaller sample size. In addition, because of substantial advance knowledge of respondent characteristics, population-based experiments make blocking to increase the efficiency of the experimental design highly feasible.

But as with any research approach, it is risky to draw conclusions about external validity based purely on the type of research method that is being used. Judgments about the generalizability of population-based experiments must be made on a study by study basis because external validity involves more than just a real world setting. The diversity of participants within population-based experiments typically lends these studies greater external validity with respect to study participants than most laboratory or field experiments. Likewise, the study environment is more naturalistic than most laboratory settings. But for the most part, no more is known about the external validity of treatments and measures in this type of study than in any other kind of study. It is up to scholars who care a great deal about the generalizability of findings to incorporate evidence of these kinds of external validity in future population-based survey experiments.

---

[50] Some survey experiments have used techniques for administering treatments that easily allow noncompliance, a practice I do not recommend (e.g., Horiuchi, Imai, and Taniguchi, 2007). Due to the lack of control over assignment to conditions, these studies essentially become more like field experiments as a result of selection effects.

More Than Just Another Method

I ADMIT TO TAKING a certain perverse delight in finding out that some "consensus knowledge" is actually misguided. Sugary breakfast cereals improve kids' test scores,[1] gentrification attracts minorities,[2] and despite slang to the contrary, humans are the only primates who lack penis bones.[3] Likewise, one of the pleasant side-benefits of population-based survey experiments is that they turn on their head some of the "truisms" learned about research methods while in graduate school. There is no necessary trade-off between internal and external validity in the choice of a research design. Experiments can be useful in evaluating generalizability. Covariates are not always your friends.

Ultimately, though, cheap thrills cannot sustain a methodology. The only thing that will accomplish this is strong, theoretically important work. As the many examples in this volume attest, there is already a good start in this general direction. But because they *can* be used toward these ends does not mean that they necessarily will be. This book can be thought of as an extended public service advertisement meant to ensure the continued development of this kind of work.

By the time readers reach this final chapter, my hope is that they will be convinced that population-based experiments have a place in the methods arsenal of social scientists. Population-based experiments are not a panacea for all that ails observational and experimental methods, but currently they are an under-utilized methodological approach with the potential to strengthen the social sciences.

Perhaps more importantly, the concept of population-based experiments has the capacity to encourage innovation and change how social scientists think about research design. The possibilities have only begun to be tapped. My expectation is that this book will be replaced in a few years by a much thicker and more extensive consideration of the use and

---

[1] See Mahoney, Taylor, Kanarek, and Samuel (2005); Kleinman (1994).
[2] McKinnish, Walsh, and White (2010).
[3] For theoretical explanations, see Sarma and Weilbaecher (1990); Champion and Wegrzyn (1964); Dawkins (2006); Gilbert and Zevit (2001).

development of population-based experiments, a volume that embodies design ideas and treatment methods that have not yet been conceived.

In addition to improving the empirical bases of social scientific knowledge, population-based survey experiments may help to break down many of the longstanding misconceptions regarding survey and experimental research methods. Scholars who combine random assignment to experimental conditions with representative samples of subjects are forced to reconsider the accepted wisdom about the strengths and weaknesses of these typically distinct paradigms.

As it turns out, it is not as simple as each being strong at the other's weaknesses. The combination of the two approaches offers some advantages that are unique to population-based experiments, as well as some hurdles. On the positive side, scholars can reap benefits from the ability to generalize an experimental causal inference to a representative sample of the precise population to which a given theory is supposed to apply. Medical researchers would kill[4] for the opportunity to estimate population average treatment effects for interventions designed to reduce mortality. Yet they are usually stuck with results from unrepresentative clinical trials.

Social scientists, by comparison, are fortunate that many of their treatments can ethically be applied to a representative sample. What they can accomplish thereby goes far beyond more accurate quantification of average treatment effects. Social scientists have the opportunity to establish the boundaries of important theories. By integrating concerns about internal and external validity, population-based experiments help to allay the impression that the two forms of validity are incompatible, mutually exclusive qualities.

As noted, the opportunities offered by this method are not without their challenges. The first of these problems is to find population-based treatments that are both effective and ethical. But as the studies in this volume attest, with creativity it can often be accomplished. No one could convincingly argue that this approach is a desirable way to test all theories, but population-based experiments present new opportunities that will only become more extensive with time and technological advances. Moreover, as the proportion of the population that is reachable via networking technologies increases and approaches full coverage in the United States, the costs of research of this kind should decline precipitously. In the longer term, access will extend to the rest of the world as well. Future possibilities for cross-national and cross-cultural experimentation are exciting to ponder.

---

[4] The Hippocratic Oath fortunately forbids this.

Because of its tremendous long-term potential, scholars should proceed carefully to preserve access to this method for future researchers. Telephone access to random population samples has become endangered as a research tool largely because this access was used for unscrupulous as well as scrupulous ends. It would be a serious loss to the scientific community if the reputation of Internet-based research proceeded down the same path. Careful delineation of scholarly research (as opposed to telemarketing) and adherence to recognizable protocols and ethical standards will be necessary to prevent this form of research from the kind of disrepute that telephone surveys have experienced from the public's inability to distinguish between scientific research and telemarketing or political "push polling."

I have tried to point out the limitations of this approach in the preceding chapters, but it would be a mistake to infer from this that population-based experiments are "just another method" in the social scientist's armory, with the same balance of strengths and weaknesses. Relative to traditional methods—laboratory experiments, field experiments, quasi-experiments, observational studies, and surveys—population-based experiments have an usually rich collection of advantages, combined with very few of the disadvantages of these other useful approaches. In fact, population-based experiments come closest to what has been termed the "ideal experiment,"[5] that is, the kind of study that combines random selection of subjects from the population of interest with random assignment to experimental treatments.

By simultaneously ensuring internal validity and maximizing the capacity for external validity, population-based experiments may be unmatched in their ability to advance social scientific knowledge. For ethical and/or technical reasons, it may not be possible to implement them in all circumstances, but given their many advantages, it is well worth the time and effort to develop still more creative and innovative ways to implement population-based experiments.

In some ways, population-based experiments could be considered an "easy publication" because even if the study is a "mere replication" of a previous laboratory study, or an observational study, it still has obvious value-added. Its contribution to knowledge could be that it demonstrates that laboratory findings are generalizable to a more diverse population. Better yet, if it is a replication of an observational study of some kind, then its contribution to knowledge is solidifying (or not) the causal nature of a previously suggested relationship.

---

[5] See Imai, King, and Stuart (2008).

A cynic might therefore say that it requires relatively little creativity to publish this type of work; borrow someone else's theories and off you go. This characterization overlooks some of the central challenges facing those who wish to execute a population-based survey experiment. Because of the tremendous variance in the experimental sample, significant effects are far harder to come by than in the lab. Moreover, experimental treatments are more difficult to implement as well. The ability to use experiments to potentially improve both internal and external validity within a single study is unique, but the price is far more forethought in both design and execution.

To date, the contributions of this methodological approach cannot rival those of other well-known methods such as surveys, experiments, and field experiments; there are simply too few such studies thus far, and the method remains in its infancy. Nonetheless, I anticipate that population-based survey experiments will contribute substantially in the next twenty years, not only to theory-testing, but also to much greater knowledge of the boundaries of those theories.

THE ROLE OF POPULATION-BASED SURVEY EXPERIMENTS

Almost all experiments involve research focused on a causal process of some kind. But it is worth noting that not all studies are deeply concerned about external validity writ large. Most of what has been said in this book applies to what are known as "universalistic" research purposes; that is, when investigators want to know about theoretically predicted causal relationships between abstract concepts. For example, does gender influence status? Does social trust influence economic development?[6] The boundaries of universalistic theories are seldom explicitly stated nor implied, so generalizability remains an important question to be explored empirically.

But when conducting population-based experiments in order to obtain results that are policy-relevant, especially with the explicit purpose of influencing policymakers, population-based survey experiments can be especially valuable to more particularistic research because the target of applicability is known and specified. There are many important particularistic research goals that incorporate boundaries for generalizability within the research question itself. For example, could the butterfly ballot used in the 2000 presidential election for voting in Palm Beach County, Florida, have caused people who intended to vote for Al Gore to vote for Pat Buchanan instead? In this case, the setting, the treatment, the outcome measure, and

---

[6] For details on this distinction, consult Hoyle, Harris, and Judd (2002).

the population of interest are all embedded within the research question itself. The question is obviously important, and the answer appears to be yes.[7] With particularistic research questions such as this one, population-based survey experiments are important not so much to explore boundaries of generalizability as to establish that the empirical cause and effect relationship works as predicted on the targeted population.

The role of population-based survey experiments in testing more universalistic theories is one of establishing boundaries. It may be well-established that X causes Y from laboratory studies, but population-based experiments can tell us that X causes Y with certain kinds of people in certain kinds of situations. I have sensed at times that many scholars would prefer not to know the boundaries of their theories. Although establishing the boundaries within which a given theory should be expected to work is a genuine advance in scientific knowledge, it often feels more like a limitation or a setback. Inconsistent research findings can lead to useful revisions of a theory, but consistent findings are far easier to interpret and publish.

Establishing theoretical boundaries is an undervalued enterprise, and thus it is understandable why certain patterns of scholarship emerge. A given type of study produces reliable findings, so the same treatment, the same measures, and the same study design get used over and over. Failures to replicate are viewed with suspicion (and are difficult to publish). This understandable cautiousness leads to lots of replication, but also to little or no understanding of the boundaries of any given theory. But in reality, a theory with known boundaries is not an inferior theory; in fact, it is actually preferable to one with unknown boundaries. Unfortunately, the academic system tends to value universal theory over theories with known boundaries, and thus it tends not to value null or variable findings to the extent it ought to.[8]

By increasing the variety of experimental subjects, the settings in which research is done, and the kinds of treatments and measures that are utilized, population-based survey experiments may produce greater awareness of the boundaries of various social science theories. Whether this kind of activity is welcome or not, it remains an important contribution to social science knowledge. Realistically, it should come as no surprise that truly universal theories are hard to come by when studying organisms as multifaceted as human beings embedded in complex social systems.

Beyond producing contributions to scientific knowledge, I expect that this approach will contribute to reconsiderations of how scholars teach and think about internal and external validity. There is nothing about the

---

[7] See Sinclair et al. (2000).
[8] See Gerber et al. (2010) for an example of the consequences of publication bias.

laboratory setting that guarantees internal validity—only random assignment has the ability to do that. Likewise, there is nothing about a field setting that guarantees external validity. Only studies that purposely include diverse populations of subjects, as well as variations in settings, treatments, and outcome measures can accomplish this. It is time for research methods textbooks to abandon the idea, embedded in most introductory textbooks, that there must be a trade-off between external and internal validity in choice of research method.

Abelson, R. P. 1995. *Statistics as Principled Argument.* Hillsdale, NJ: Lawrence Erlbaum Associates.

Ackerman, B., and J. Fishkin. 2004. *Deliberation Day.* New Haven, CT: Yale University Press.

Ahart, A. M., and P. R. Sackett. 2004. A new method of examining relationship between individual difference measures and sensitive behavior criteria: Evaluating the unmatched count technique. *Organizational Research Methods* 7:101–14.

Alpizar, F., F. Carlsson, and O. Johansson-Stenman. 2008. Does context matter more for hypothetical than for actual contributions? Evidence from a natural field experiment. *Experimental Economics* 11:299–314.

Anderson, C. A., and B. J. Bushman. 1997. External validity of "trivial" experiments: The case of laboratory aggression. *Review of General Psychology* 1(1):19–41.

Asch, S. 1952. *Social Psychology.* Englewood Cliffs, NJ: Prentice-Hall.

Avant, D., and L. Sigelman. 2006. Globalization, private security, and the democratic peace. In *Globalization and Transatlantic Security*, ed. R. A. Epstein and P. Vennesson, 7–32. Florence, Italy: European University Institute.

——. 2008. What does private security in Iraq mean for democracy at home? http://www.international.ucla.edu/burkle/podcasts/article.asp?parentid=86477 (accessed August 17, 2009).

Bailenson, J. N., S. Iyengar, N. Yee, and N. A. Collins. 2008. Facial similarity between voters and candidates causes influence. *Public Opinion Quarterly* 72(5):935–61.

Barabas, J., and J. Jerit. 2008. The external validity of treatments: A comparison of natural and survey experiments. Paper presented at the annual meeting of the Midwest Political Science Association, Chicago, IL.

Barabas, J., and J. Jerit. 2010. Are survey experiments externally valid? *American Political Science Review* 104(2): 226–242.

Battalio, R. C., J. H. Kagel, and M. O. Reynolds. 1977. Income distributions in two experimental economies. *Journal of Political Economy* 85(6):1259–71.

Benz, M., and S. Meier. 2008. Do people behave in experiments as in the field? Evidence from donations. *Experimental Economics* 11:268–81.

Berkowitz, L., and E. Donnerstein. 1982. External validity is more than skin deep: Some answers to criticisms of laboratory experiments. *American Psychologist* 37(3):245–57.

Bohnet, I., and R. Zeckhauser. 2004a. Trust, risk and betrayal. *Journal of Economic Behavior and Organization* 55:467–84.

——. 2004b. Trust and risk. Proposal to TESS. http://tess.experimentcentral.org/data/bohnet192.html (accessed February 11, 2010).

Bonetti, S. 1998. Experimental economics and deception. *Journal of Economic Psychology* 19(3):377–95.

Bowers, J. 2010. Making effects manifest: How can we enhance the sensitivity of experiments using what we (think we) know. In *Handbook of Experimental Political Science*, ed. J. Druckman, D. Green, J. Kuklinski, and A. Lupia. New York, NY: Cambridge University Press.

Brown, N. R., and R. C. Sinclair. 1999. Estimating number of lifetime sexual partners: Men and women do it differently. *Journal of Sex Research* 36:292–97.

Brueckner, H., A. Morning, and A. Nelson. 2005. The expression of biological concepts of race. Paper presented at the annual meeting of the American Sociological Association, Philadelphia, PA.

Buss, D. M. 2000. *The Dangerous Passion: Why Jealousy Is as Necessary as Love and Sex*. New York, NY: Free Press.

Buss, D. M., R. J. Larsen, D. Westen, and J. Semmelroth. 1992. Sex differences in jealousy: Evolution, physiology, and psychology. *Psychological Science* 3(4):251–55.

Buss, D. M., T. K. Shackelford, L. A. Kirkpatrick, J. C. Choe, H. K. Lim, M. Hasegawa, T. Hasegawa, and K. Bennett. 1999. Jealousy and the nature of beliefs about infidelity: Tests of competing hypotheses about sex differences in the United States, Korea, and Japan. *Personal Relationships* 6:121–50.

Buunk, B. P., A. Angleitner, V. Oubaid, and D. M. Buss. 1996. Sex differences in jealousy in evolutionary and cultural perspective: Tests from the Netherlands, Germany, and the United States. *Psychological Science* 7:359–63.

Cao, X. 2010. Pathways to eliciting aid: The effects of visual representations of human suffering on empathy and help for people in need. Dissertation presented February 16, University of Pennsylvania, Annenberg School for Communication.

Campbell, D. T., and J. C. Stanley. 1963. *Experimental and Quasi-Experimental Designs for Research*. Chicago, IL: Rand McNally.

Carpenter, J., C. Connolly, and C. K. Myers. 2008. Altruistic behavior in a representative dictator experiment. *Experimental Economics* 11:282–98.

Castronova, E., M. W. Bell, M. Carlton, R. Cornell, J. J. Cummings, W. Emigh, M. Falk, M. Fatten, P. LaFourest, N. Mishler, J. Reynard, S. Robbins, T. Ross, W. Ryan, and R. Starks. 2008. A test of the law of demand in a virtual world: Exploring the Petri dish approach to social science. CESifo Working Paper No. 2355.

Champion, R. H., and J. Wegrzyn. 1964. Congenital os penis. *Journal of Urology* 91(June):663–64.

Chang, L., and J. A. Krosnick. 2009. National surveys via RDD telephone interviewing versus the Internet: Comparing sample representativeness and response quality. *Public Opinion Quarterly* 73(4):641–78.

Chesney, T., S. Chuah, and R. Hoffmann. 2009. Virtual world experimentation: An exploratory study. *Journal of Economic Behavior and Organization* 72:618–35.

Cohen, B. P. 1989. *Developing Sociological Knowledge: Theory and Method*. Chicago, IL: Nelson-Hall.

———. 1997. Beyond experimental inference: A decent burial for J.S. Mill and R.A. Fisher. In *Status, Network, and Structure: Theory Development in Group*

Processes, ed. J. Szmatka, J. Skvoretz, and J. Berger, 71–86. Palo Alto, CA: Stanford University Press.

Conley, D. A. 2006. From the eye of the beholder: Attitudes about physical attractiveness and their social and demographic correlates. Summary for TESS website. http://tess.experimentcentral.org/data/conley466.html.

Conley, D. A., and R. Glauber. 2005. Gender, body mass, and economic status. *National Bureau of Economic Research*: Cambridge, MA, Working Paper No. w11343.

Cook, T. D., and D. T. Campbell. 1976. The design and conduct of quasi-experiments and true experiments in field settings. In *Handbook of Industrial and Organizational Psychology*, ed. M. Dunnette. Chicago, IL: Rand McNally.

Cook, T. D., and D. T. Campbell. 1979. *Quasi-Experimentation: Design & Analysis Issues for Field Settings*. Boston, MA: Houghton-Mifflin.

Corrigan, P. W., and A. C. Watson. 2007. The stigma of psychiatric disorders and the gender, ethnicity, and education of the perceiver. *Community Mental Health Journal* 43(5):439–58.

Corrigan, P. W., A. C. Watson, and F. E. Miller. 2006. Blame, shame, and contamination: The impact of mental illness and drug dependence stigma on family members. *Journal of Family Psychology* 20(2):239–46.

Corstange, D. 2009. Sensitive questions, truthful answers? Modeling the list experiment with LISTIT. *Political Analysis* 17(1):45–63.

Cottrell, C. A., and S. L. Neuberg. 2005. Different emotional reactions to different groups: A sociofunctional threat-based approach to "prejudice." *Journal of Personality and Social Psychology* 88(5):770–89.

Darley, J. M., and L. M. Solan. 2005. Moral luck, loss of chance, and legal liability. Summary for TESS website. http://tess.experimentcentral.org/data/darley324.html (accessed August 17, 2009).

Darley, J. M., L. M. Solan, M. B. Kugler, and J. Sanders. 2007. Liability for risk: Citizens' perspectives on liability for creation of risk and loss of chance. 2nd Annual Conference on Empirical Legal Studies Paper (October). Available at SSRN: http://ssrn.com/abstract=998641.

Davis, M. M., and K. Fant. 2005. Coverage of vaccines in private health plans: What does the public prefer? *Health Affairs* 24(3):770–79.

Davis, M. M., and D. Singer. 2006. After the storms: Anticipated effects of gasoline prices on health behaviors and health-related consumption. Summary for TESS website. http://tess.experimentcentral.org/data/davis471.html.

Dawkins, R. 2006. *The Selfish Gene: 30th Anniversary Edition*. Oxford, UK: Oxford University Press.

Dipboye, R. L., and M. F. Flanagan. 1979. Research settings in industrial and organizational psychology: Are findings in the field more generalizable than in the laboratory? *American Psychologist* 34(2):141–50.

Dougherty, C. 2007. Bragg v. Linden: Virtual property rights litigation. *E-Commerce Law & Policy* 9(7). Available at SSRN: http://ssrn.com/abstract=1092284.

Druckman, J. N., and C. D. Kam. 2010. Students as experimental participants: A defense of the "narrow data base." In *Handbook of Experimental Political*

Science, ed. J. Druckman, D. Green, J. Kuklinski, and A. Lupia. New York, NY: Cambridge University Press.

Eaton, A. A., and P. S. Visser. 2008. The effects of gender and power on persuasion. Paper presented at the annual meeting of the Midwestern Psychological Association, Chicago, IL.

Eisenberger, N. I., M. D. Lieberman, and K. D. Williams. 2003. Does rejection hurt? An fMRI study of social exclusion. *Science* 302:290-92.

Evans, S. H., and E. J. Anastasio. 1968. Misuse of analysis of covariance when treatment effect and covariate are confounded. *Psychological Bulletin* 69(4):225-34.

Feld, S. L., and R. B. Felson. 2008. Gender norms and retaliatory violence against spouses and acquaintances. *Journal of Family Issues* 29(5):692-703.

Firebaugh, G. 2008. *Seven Rules for Social Research*. Princeton, NJ: Princeton University Press.

Fischer, R. A. 1935. *The Design of Experiments*. London, UK: Oliver and Boyd.

———. 1956. *Statistical Methods and Scientific Inference*. Edinburgh, UK: Oliver and Boyd.

Fong, C. M., and E. F. P. Luttmer. 2009. What determines giving to Hurricane Katrina victims? Experimental evidence on racial group loyalty. *American Economic Journal: Applied Economics* 1(2):64-87.

Franklin, C. 1991. Efficient estimation in experiments. *Political Methodologist* 4:13-15.

Freedman, D. 2008. On regression adjustments to experimental data. *Advances in Applied Mathematics* 40(2):180-93.

Fromkin, H. L., and S. Streufert. 1976. Laboratory experimentation. In *Handbook of Industrial and Organizational Psychology*, ed. M. D. Dunnette, 415-66. Chicago, IL: Rand McNally.

Gaines, B. J., and J. H. Kuklinski. 2008. A case for including self-selection alongside randomization in the assignment of experimental treatments. Paper originally prepared for delivery at the annual meeting of the Midwest Political Science Association, Chicago, IL, September 8.

———. 2010. Treatment effects. In *Handbook of Experimental Political Science*, ed. J. Druckman, D. Green, J. Kuklinski, and A. Lupia. New York, NY: Cambridge University Press.

Gaines, B. J., J. H. Kuklinski, and P. J. Quirk. 2007. Rethinking the survey experiment. *Political Analysis* 15:1-21.

Gaylord, C. 2008. Can Web-based worlds teach us about the real one? *Christian Science Monitor*, Jan. 23, p. 13. http://www.csmonitor.com/Innovation/Tech/2008/0123/p13s01-stct.html (accessed October 30, 2009).

Gerber, A. S., and D. P. Green. 2000a. The effects of canvassing, direct mail, and telephone contact on voter turnout: A field experiment. *American Political Science Review* 94:653-63.

———. 2000b. The effect of a nonpartisan get-out-the-vote drive: An experimental study of leafletting. *Journal of Politics* 62(3):846-57.

———. 2001. Do phone calls increase voter turnout? A field experiment. *Public Opinion Quarterly* 65:75-85.

Gerber, A. S., D. P. Green, and C. W. Larimer. 2008. Social pressure and voter turn-out: Evidence from a large-scale field experiment. *American Political Science Review* 102(1):33–48.

Gerber, A. S., D. P. Green, and R. Shachar. 2003. Voting may be habit forming: Evidence from a randomized field experiment. *American Journal of Political Science* 47(3):540–50.

Gerber, A. S., N. Malhotra, C. M. Dowling, and D. Dohert. 2010. Publication bias in two political behavior literatures. *American Politics Research* 38(4): 591–613.

Gilbert, S. F., and Z. Zevit. 2001. Congenital human baculum deficiency: The generative bone of Genesis 2:21–23. *American Journal of Medical Genetics* 101(3):284–85.

Gilens, M., P. M. Sniderman, and J. H. Kuklinski. 1998. Affirmative Action and the politics of realignment. *British Journal of Political Science* 28:159–83.

Gino, F., J. Shang, and R. Croson. 2009. The impact of information from similar or different advisors on judgment. *Organizational Behavior and Human Decision Processes* 108:287–302.

Goldman, S. 2008. Is it OK to be anti-gay? Social desirability, elite discourse, and expressions of intolerance. Paper presented at the annual meeting of the Midwest Political Science Association, Chicago, IL, April 3.

Gonsalkorale, K., and K. D. Williams. 2007. The KKK won't let me play: Ostracism even by a despised outgroup hurts. *European Journal of Social Psychology* 37:1176–1186.

Graham, S. M., and M. S. Clark. 2006. Self-esteem and organization of valenced information about others: The "Jekyll and Hyde"-ing of relationship partners. *Journal of Personality and Social Psychology* 90(4):652–65.

Green, D. P., and A. S. Gerber. 2003. The underprovision of experiments in political science. *ANNALS of the American Academy of Political and Social Science* 589(1):94–112.

———. 2004. *Get Out the Vote! How to Increase Voter Turnout.* Washington, DC: Brookings Institution.

Green, M. C., and J. Sabini. 2006. Gender, socioeconomic status, age, and jealousy: Emotional responses to infidelity in a national sample. *Emotion* 6(2): 330–34.

Hansen, B. B., and J. Bowers. 2008. Covariate balance in simple, stratified and clustered comparative studies. *Statistical Science* 23(2):219–36.

Horiuchi, Y., K. Imai, and N. Taniguchi. 2007. Designing and analyzing randomized experiments: Application to a Japanese election survey experiment. *American Journal of Political Science* 51(3):669–87.

Hoyle, R. H., M. J. Harris, and C. M. Judd. 2002. *Research Methods in Social Relations* (7th ed.). Pacific Grove, CA: Wadsworth Publishing.

Holbrook, A., and J. A. Krosnick. 2004. Vote over-reporting: A test of the social desirability hypothesis. Paper presented at the annual meeting of the American Association for Public Opinion Research, Phoenix, AZ.

Holland, P. W. 1986. Statistics and causal inference. *Journal of the American Statistical Association* 81 (396):945–60.

Hopkins, D., and G. King. 2010. Improving anchoring vignettes: Designing surveys to correct interpersonal incomparability. *Public Opinion Quarterly* 74(2):201–22.

Hovland, C. I. 1959. Reconciling conflicting results derived from experimental and survey studies of attitude change. *American Psychologist* 14(1):8–17.

Huber, M., L. Van Boven, B. Park, and W. Pizzi. 2006. Reactions to Hurricane Katrina: Political polarization, emotions, and stereotypes. Poster presented at Human and Social Dynamics Principal Investigators Meeting, National Science Foundation, Washington, DC.

———. 2007. Politically polarized evaluations of the Bush administration's response to Hurricane Katrina. Poster presented at Society for Personality and Social Psychology, Memphis, TN.

Hutchings, V., H. Walton, Jr., and A. Benjamin. 2005. Heritage or hate? Race, gender, partisanship, and the Georgia state flag controversy. Paper presented at the annual meeting of the American Political Science Association, Washington, DC.

Ilgen, D. R. 1986. Laboratory research: A question of when, not if. In *Generalizing From Laboratory to Field Settings: Research Findings From Industrial-Organizational Psychology, Organizational Behavior, and Human Resource Management*, ed. E. A. Locke, 257–67. Lexington, MA: Lexington Books.

Imai, K., G. King, and E. A. Stuart. 2008. Misunderstandings among experimentalists and observationalists about causal inference. *Journal of the Royal Statistical Society, Series A* 171, Part 2, 481–502.

Iyengar, S. 1987. Television news and citizens' explanations of national affairs. *American Political Science Review* 81(3):815–31.

Iyengar, S., and D. R. Kinder. 1987. *News That Matters: Television and American Opinion.* Chicago, IL: University of Chicago Press.

Jamison, J., D. S. Karlan, and L. Schechter. 2006. To deceive or not to deceive: The effect of deception on behavior in future laboratory experiments. Yale Economic Applications and Policy Discussion Paper No. 18 (June). Available at SSRN: http://ssrn.com/abstract=913057.

Janus, A. L. 2006. The list experiment as an unobtrusive measure of attitudes toward immigration and same-sex marriages. Summary for TESS website. http://tess.experimentcentral.org/data/janus297.html (accessed February 11, 2010).

Kane, J. G., S. C. Craig, and K. D. Wald. 2004. Religion and presidential politics in Florida: A list experiment. *Social Science Quarterly* 85:281–93.

Kelman, H. C. 1967. Human use of human subjects: The problem of deception in social psychological experiments. *Psychological Bulletin* 67(1):1–11.

Kinder, D. R. 2007. Curmudgeonly advice. *Journal of Communication* 57:155–62.

Kinder, D. R., and T. R. Palfrey. 1993. On behalf of an experimental political science. In *Experimental Foundations of Political Science*, ed. D. R. Kinder and T. R. Palfrey, 1–42. Ann Arbor, MI: University of Michigan Press.

King, G., C. J. L. Murray, J. A. Salomon, and A. Tandon. 2004. Enhancing the validity and cross-cultural comparability of measurement in survey research. *American Political Science Review* 98(1):191–207.

King, G., and J. Wand. 2007. Comparing incomparable survey responses: New tools for anchoring vignettes. *Political Analysis* 15(1):46–66.

Kleinman, Robert E. 1994. *Let Them Eat Cake! The Case Against Controlling What Your Children Eat.* New York, NY: Villard Books.

Knowles, M. L., and W. L. Gardner. 2006. Parasocial "friendships" among individuals with dispositionally high belonging needs. Paper presented at the annual meeting of the Midwestern Psychological Association, Chicago, IL.

Kosova, W., and P. Wingert. 2009. Crazy talk, Oprah, wacky cures and you. *Newsweek Magazine*, June 8.

Krasno, J. S., and D. P. Green. 2008. Do televised presidential ads increase voter turnout? Evidence from a natural experiment. *Journal of Politics* 70(1):245–61.

Kuklinski, J. H., M. D. Cobb, and M. Gilens. 1997. Racial attitudes and the "new South." *Journal of Politics* 59(2):323–49.

Lasorsa, D.L. 2006. Effects of the subjective experiment of knowledge difficulty on self-judgment of political interest. Paper presented at the annual convention of the Association for Education in Journalism and Mass Communication, San Francisco, CA.

Levitt, S. D., and J. A. List. 2007. What do laboratory experiments measuring social preferences reveal about the real world? *Journal of Economic Perspectives* 21(2):153–74.

Li, K. 2009. TV ratings shake-up challenges Nielsen. *Financial Times*, August 13.

Liyanarachchi, G. A. 2007. Feasibility of using student subjects in accounting experiments: A review. *Pacific Accounting Review* 19(1):47–67.

Locke, E. A. 1986. Generalizing from laboratory to field: Ecological validity or abstraction of essential elements? In *Generalizing From Laboratory to Field Settings: Research Findings From Industrial-Organizational Psychology, Organizational Behavior, and Human Resource Management*, ed. E. A. Locke, 3–9. Lexington, MA: Lexington Books.

Loftus, T. 2005. Virtual worlds wind up in real world's courts. Feb. 7. http://www.msnbc.msn.com/id/6870901/ (accessed February 23, 2010).

Mahoney, C. R., H. A. Taylor, R. B. Kanarek, and P. Samuel. 2005. Effect of breakfast composition on cognitive processes in elementary school children. *Physiology & Behavior* 85:635–45.

Malhotra, N., A. J. Healy, and C. H. Mo. 2009 (July 11). Personal emotions and political decision making: Implications for voter competence. Stanford University Graduate School of Business Research Paper No. 2034. Available at SSRN: http://ssrn.com/abstract=1447502 (accessed January 11, 2010).

Malhotra, N., and A. G. Kuo. 2008. Attributing blame: The public's response to Hurricane Katrina. *Journal of Politics* 70(1):120–35.

———. 2009. Emotions as moderators of information cue use: Citizen attitudes towards Hurricane Katrina. *American Politics Research* 37(2):301–26.

Marsh, C. 1982. *The Survey Method: The Contribution of Surveys to Sociological Explanation.* London, UK: George Allen and Unwin.

McKinnish, T., R. Walsh, and T. K. White. 2010. Who gentrifies low-income neighborhoods? *Journal of Urban Economics* 67(2):169–248.

Mill, J. S. 1843. *A System of Logic, Ratiocinative and Inductive, Being a Connected View of the Principles of Evidence, and the Methods of Scientific Investigation,* Vol. 1. London, UK: John W. Parker, West Strand.

Mintz, A., S. B. Redd, and A. Vedlitz. 2006. Can we generalize from student experiments to the real world in political science, military affairs, and international relations? *Journal of Conflict Resolution* 50:757-76.

Mollborn, S. 2005. Measuring teenage pregnancy norms and their effect on resource provision. Summary for TESS website. http://tess.experimentcentral .org/data/mollborn390.html (accessed February 11, 2010).

———. 2009. Norms about nonmarital pregnancy and willingness to provide resources to unwed parents. *Journal of Marriage and Family* 71:122-34.

Mutz, D. C. 1992. Impersonal influence: Effects of representations of public opinion on political attitudes. *Political Behavior* 14(2):89-122.

———. 1998. *Impersonal influence: How Perceptions of Mass Collectives Affect Political Attitudes.* Cambridge, UK: Cambridge University Press.

———. 2002. Cross-cutting social networks: Testing democratic theory in practice. *American Political Science Review* 96(2):111-26.

———. 2005. Social trust and e-commerce: Experimental evidence for the effects of social trust on individual economic behavior. *Public Opinion Quarterly* 69(3):393-416.

———. 2009. Effects of Internet commerce on social trust. *Public Opinion Quarterly* 73(3):439-61.

———. 2010. The dog that didn't bark: The role of canines in the 2008 presidential campaign. *PS: Political Science and Politics* 43(4): 707-12.

Mutz, D. C., and R. Pemantle. 2011. *The Perils of Randomization Checks in the Analysis of Experiments.* Philadelphia, PA: University of Pennsylvania. Preprint.

O'Keefe, D. J. 2003. Message properties, mediating states, and manipulation checks: Claims, evidence, and data analysis in experimental persuasive message effects research. *Communication Theory* 13(3):251-74.

Oliver, J. E. 2005. *Fat Politics: The Real Story Behind America's Obesity Epidemic.* New York, NY: Oxford University Press.

Oliver, J. E., and T. Lee. 2005. Public opinion and the politics of obesity. *Journal of Health Politics, Policy and Law* 30(5):923-54.

Omodei, M. M., and A. J. Wearing. 1995. The Fire Chief microworld generating program: An illustration of computer-simulated microworlds as an experimental paradigm for studying complex decision-making behavior. *Behavior Research Methods, Instruments, & Computers* 27:303-16.

Ostfeld, M., and D. C. Mutz. 2010. *Revisiting the Effects of Personalization: American Attitudes toward Immigration Policy.* Manuscript under review.

Pager, D., and J. Freese. 2004. Who deserves a helping hand? Attitudes about government assistance for the unemployed by race, incarceration status, and worker history. Paper presented at the annual meeting of the American Sociological Association, San Francisco, CA.

Panagopoulos, C., and D. P. Green. 2008. Field experiments testing the impact of radio advertisements on electoral competition. *American Journal of Political Science* 52(1):156-68.

Penny, M. 2006. The perceptual basis of social organization. Unpublished manuscript. http://www.wjh.harvard.edu/~mpenny/Perceptual_Basis_06.pdf (accessed February 23, 2010).

Penny, M., and W. J. Wilson. 2006. Perceiving neighborhoods: Exploring the effects of subjective evaluations on the process of social organization. Summary for TESS website. http://tess.experimentcentral.org/data/penny489.html (accessed February 22, 2010).

Peterson, R. A., G. Albaum, and R. F. Beltramini. 1985. A meta-analysis of effect sizes in consumer behavior experiments. *Journal of Consumer Research* 12:97-103.

Pettigrew, T. F., and L. R. Tropp. 2006. A meta-analytic test of intergroup contact theory. *Journal of Personality and Social Psychology* 90(5):751-83.

Piazza, T., P. M. Sniderman, and P. E. Tetlock. 1989. Analysis of the dynamics of political reasoning: A general purpose computer-assisted methodology. In *Political Analysis*, ed. J. Stimson, vol. 1, 99-120. Ann Arbor, Mich.: University of Michigan Press.

Pocock, S. J., S. E. Assmann, L. E. Enos, and L. E. Kasten. 2002. Subgroup analysis, covariate adjustment and baseline comparisons in clinical trial reporting: Current practice and problems. *Statistics in Medicine* 21(19):2917-2930.

Prior, M. 2006. Does self-reported news exposure measure political interest, not actual exposure? Summary for TESS website. http://tess.experimentcentral .org/data/prior348.html (accessed February 22, 2010).

———. 2009. Improving media effects research through better measurement of news exposure. *Journal of Politics* 71(3):893-908.

Pryor, J. B., and J. Ernst. 2005. The roots of sexual prejudice. Summary for TESS website. http://tess.experimentcentral.org/data/pryor283.html (accessed February 11, 2010).

Rashotte, L., and M. Webster. 2005a. Gender status beliefs. *Social Science Research* 34:618-33.

———. 2005b. Status effects of gender. Summary for TESS website. http://tess .experimentcentral.org/data/rashotte392.html (accessed August 17, 2009).

Rasinski, K. A., P. S. Visser, M. Zagatsky, and E. M. Rickett. 2005. Using implicit goal priming to improve the quality of self-report data. *Journal of Experimental Social Psychology* 41:321-27.

Robinson, P. H., and R. Kurzban. 2006. Do people agree on how much punishment fits crimes? Summary for TESS website. http://tess.experimentcentral .org/data/kurzban506.html (accessed August 17, 2009).

———. 2007. Concordance and conflict in intuitions of justice. *Minnesota Law Review* 91 (6):1829-1907.

Ross, L., G. Bierbrauer, and S. Hoffman. 1976. The role of attribution processes in conformity and dissert: Revisiting the Asch situation. *American Psychologist* 31:148-57.

Ross, L., and R. E. Nisbett. 1991. *The Person and The Situation*. New York, NY: McGraw-Hill.

Sabini, J., and M. Silver. 2005. Gender and jealousy: Stories of infidelity. *Cognition and Emotion* 19(5):713-27.

Sarma, D., and T. Weilbaecher. 1990. Human os penis. *Urology* 35:349–50.

Schaeffer, N. C. 1991. Hardly ever or constantly? Group comparisons using vague quantifiers. *Public Opinion Quarterly* 55:395–423.

Schwarz, N., and G. L. Clore. 1983. Mood, misattribution, and judgments of well-being: Informative and directive functions of affective states. *Journal of Personality and Social Psychology* 45(3):513–23.

Sears, D. O. 1986. College sophomores in the laboratory: Influences of a narrow data base on social psychology's view of human nature. *Journal of Personality and Social Psychology* 51(3):515–30.

Sekhon, J. S. 2009. Combining experimental and observational data to estimate population treatment effects: New methods and the case of pulmonary artery catheterization. Colloquium presented to the Statistics Department, University of Pennsylvania, December 2, Philadelphia, PA.

Senn, S. 1994. Testing for baseline balance in clinical trials. *Statistics in Medicine* 13(17):1715–1726.

Shadish, W. R., Cook, T. D., and D. T. Campbell. 2002. *Experimental and Quasi-Experimental Designs for Generalized Causal Inference.* Boston, MA: Houghton-Mifflin.

Shaker, L. K., and E. N. Ben-Porath. 2010. News images, race, and attribution in the wake of Hurricane Katrina. *Journal of Communication.* Volume 60(3): 466–490.

Sinclair, R. C., M. M. Mark, S. E. Moore, C. A. Lavis, and A.S. Soldat. 2000. Psychology: An electoral butterfly effect. *Nature* 408(6813):665–66.

Sinclair, R. C., and S. E. Moore. 2006. Estimating number of lifetime sexual partners: A strategy activation study. Summary for TESS website. http://tess .experimentcentral.org/data/sinclair320.html (accessed February 19, 2010).

Singer, E., J. Van Hoewyk, and M. P. Maher. 2000. Experiments with incentives in telephone surveys. *Public Opinion Quarterly* 64:171–88.

Sniderman, P. M., and E. G. Carmines. 1997. *Reaching Beyond Race.* Cambridge, MA: Harvard University Press.

Sniderman, P. M., and D. B. Grob. 1996. Innovations in experimental design in attitude surveys. *Annual Review of Sociology* 22:377–99.

Sniderman, P. M., and T. Piazza. 1993. *The Scar of Race.* Cambridge, MA: Harvard University Press.

Sniderman, P. M., T. Piazza, P. E. Tetlock, and A. Kendrick. 1991. The new racism. *American Journal of Political Science* 35(2):423–47.

Sniderman, P. M., and S. M. Theriault. 2004. The structure of political argument and the logic of issue framing. In *Studies in Public Opinion,* ed. W. E. Saris and P. M. Sniderman, 133–65. Princeton, NJ: Princeton University Press.

Steele, C. M. 1997. A threat in the air: How stereotypes shape intellectual identity and performance. *American Psychologist* 52(6):613–29.

Streb, M. J., B. Burrell, B. Frederick, and M. A. Genovese. 2008. Social desirability effects and support for a female American president. *Public Opinion Quarterly* 72:76–89.

Strohmeyer, R. 2005. Warcraft plague runs amok. Wired.com, Sep. 22. http://www .wired.com/gadgetlab/2005/09/warcraft_plague/ (accessed October 28, 2009).

Thye, S. 2007. Logical and philosophical foundations of experiments in the social sciences. In *Laboratory Experiments in the Social Sciences*, ed. M. Webster and J. Sell, 57–86. London, UK: Elsevier.

Todorov, A., and A. N. Mandisodza. 2004. Public opinion on foreign policy: the multilateral public that perceives itself as unilateral. *Public Opinion Quarterly* 68(3):323–48.

Tomz, M. 2007. Domestic audience costs in international relations: An experimental approach. *International Organization* 61:821–40.

Tsiatis, A. A., M. Davidian, M. Zhang, and X. Lu. 2007. Covariate adjustment for two-sample treatment comparisons in randomized clinical trials: A principled yet flexible approach. *Statistics in Medicine* 27(23):4658–4677.

Tsuchiya, T. 2005. Domain estimators for the item count technique. *Survey Methodology* 31:41–51.

Tsuchiya, T., Y. Hirai, and S. Ono. 2007. A study of the properties of the item count technique. *Public Opinion Quarterly* 71(2):253–72.

Van Beest, I., and K. D. Williams. 2006. Cyberbomb: Is it painful to be ostracized from Russian roulette? Working Paper, Department of Psychology, Leiden University.

Warren, M. E., and H. Pearse (eds.). 2008. *Designing Deliberative Democracy: The British Columbia Citizens' Assembly*. New York, NY: Cambridge University Press.

Willer, R., and N. Adams. 2008. The threat of terrorism and support for the 2008 presidential candidates: Results of a national field experiment. *Current Research in Social Psychology* 14(1):1–22.

Williams, K. D. 2007. Ostracism. *Annual Review of Psychology* 58:425–52.

Williams, K. D., and B. Jarvis. 2006. Cyberball: A program for use in research on interpersonal ostracism and acceptance. *Behavior Research Methods* 38(1): 174–80.

Williams, M. T., and E. Turkheimer. 2007. Identification and explanation of racial differences on contamination measures. *Behaviour Research and Therapy* 45:3041–3050.

Williams, M. T., E. Turkheimer, E. Magee, and T. Guterbock. 2008. The effects of race and racial priming on self-report of contamination anxiety. *Personality and Individual Differences* 44:746–57.

Wirth, J. H., and G. Bodenhausen. 2009. The role of gender in mental-illness stigma: A national experiment. *Psychological Science* 20(2):169–73.

Yeager, D. S., J. A. Krosnick, L.Chang, H. S. Javitz, M. S. Levendusky, A. Simpser, and R. Wang. 2009. Comparing the accuracy of RDD telephone surveys and Internet surveys conducted with probability and non-probability samples. http://www.knowledgenetworks.com/insights/Mode4-Probability-Based-Studies.html.

Yee, N., J. N. Bailenson, M. Urbanek, F. Chang, and D. Merget. 2007. The unbearable likeness of being digital: The persistence of nonverbal social norms in online virtual environments. *CyberPsychology and Behavior* 10(1):115–21.

Zadro, L., K. D. Williams, and R. Richardson. 2004. How low can you go? Ostracism by a computer is sufficient to lower self-reported levels of belonging, control, self-esteem, and meaningful existence. *Journal of Experimental Social Psychology* 40:560–67.

Zaller, J. 1992. *The Nature and Origins of Mass Opinion.* New York, NY: Cambridge University Press.

Zelditch, M. Jr. 2007. The external validity of experiments that test theories. In *Laboratory Experiments in the Social Sciences,* ed. M. Webster and J. Sell, 87–112. London, UK: Elsevier.

Index

Oprah. *See* Winfrey, Oprah
Ostfeld, M., 65n
ostracism, 73
over-reporting: of news exposure, 25, 33–35;
  of sexual partners, 32; of voting, 29

Pager, D., 55–56
Palfrey, T. R., 151n47
Panagopoulos, C., 145n36
panels: ongoing internet, 13, 19, 68, 95, 144;
  web-based, 92, 94
Park, B., 19n23
paternity, 42
Pearse, H., 2n3
Pemantle, R., 126n11
Penny, M., 62
personalization, 66–67
persuasion, political, 104, 140, 152
Peterson, R. A., 145n33, 149n42
Pettigrew, T. F., 136n14
Piazza, T., 4n, 17, 55n1
Pizzi, W., 19n23
Pocock, S. J., 112n6, 126n12, 127n
policy, foreign, 15, 40–42
policymakers, 20, 41, 52, 55, 79, 158
Pong, 71
power, in social context, 46, 76; lack of, 66;
  manipulating perception of, 16; and
  persuasion, 46–47; priming for, 47; and
  vulnerability, 71, 76
power, statistical, 11, 14–17, 96–97, 120–27,
  149
power, of a treatment, 73, 86, 89
pregnancy, 59–60
prejudice, 14, 28
priming, 47, 89–90
Prior, M., 34n17–18, 35n20
Pryor, J. B., 48

questions, shared demographic, 6
Quirk, P.J., 94n, 99n15

racism: individual-level measures, 30;
  new, 17
random assignment, 2–3, 10, 20, 47, 92, 100,
  109, 114–17, 134–38, 156–57; and field
  experiments, 133; and internal validity,
  22, 131, 136, 152–54; and randomization
  check 22, 110–12, 126–27
random digit dialing, 7
Rashotte, L., 11–12

Rasinski, K. A., 31
real world events, 14, 19–20, 76
realism, experimental, 60, 65, 68, 72, 75,
  134, 141–44, 150
Redd, S. B., 145n34
replication of findings, 12, 42, 110, 139,
  145–47, 157, 159
Reynolds, M. O., 78n20
Richardson, R., 73n7
risk: aversion to, 69; compensation for,
  56–57; perception of, 36, 76
Robinson, P. H., 44, 45n14
robustness: of findings, 4; of treatments, 149
Ross, L., 13n14, 141n26, 142n

Sabini, J., 43, 147n38 and 40
Sackett, P. R., 31n11
same-sex marriage, 30, 61
Samuel, P., 155n1
Sanders, J., 57n4
Sanford, M., 44
Santa Claus, xii
Sarma, D., 155n3
Schaeffer, N. C., 35n22
Schechter, L., 103n
Schwarz, N., 91n6
Sears, D. O., 11n11
Sekhon, J. S., 1n
Senn, S., 110n3
sequential data collection, 18
Shachar, R., 145n36
Shadish, W. R., 133n5
Shaker, L. K., 19n23
Shang, J., 91n8
sheep study, infamous, 45
shoplifting, 29
Sigelman, L., 40
Silver, M., 43n
Sinclair, R. C., 32, 159n7
Singer, D., 96
Singer, E., 71n
Sniderman, P. M., xi, 4n, 5, 16n18, 17, 29n3,
  55, 64n
Solan, L. M., 57
southern U.S., 28–29, 51
Spitzer, E., 43
split-ballot, 4, 21, 26
Steele, C. M., 50n22
stigma, 31, 58, 64, 67
stimulus, 47, 87, 92, 150; attention to, 13,
  85, 89; audio-visual, 88; multiple, 152;